THE
LITTLE EGG
BOOK

Jenny Ridgwell

PIATKUS

© Judy Piatkus (Publishers) Limited

First published in 1987 by
Judy Piatkus (Publishers) Limited,
5 Windmill Street, London W1P 1HF

British Library Cataloguing in Publication Data

The little egg book.
1. Cookery (Eggs)
I. Ridgwell, Jenny
641.6′75   TX745

ISBN 0-86188-675-5

Drawings by Trevor Newton
Designed by Susan Ryall
Cover photograph by John Lee

Phototypeset in 10 on 11pt Linotron Plantin by
Phoenix Photosetting, Chatham
Printed and bound in Great Britain by
The Bath Press, Avon

CONTENTS

Eggs 1
Egg Farming 5
Packing And Storing Eggs 6
Nutritional Value Of Eggs 10
Egg Rationing 12
Easter Eggs 13
Egg Games 18
Eggs And Folklore 20
Culinary Properties Of Eggs 22
Cooking With Eggs 24
Egg Recipes 30
Cooking With Other Birds' Eggs 45
Egg Drinks 48
Eggs For Beauty 50
Other Uses For Eggs 52
Tricks With Eggs 53
Did You Know. . .? 55
Eggspressions 58
Acknowledgements 59
Other Titles In The Series 60

The codfish lays 10,000 eggs,
The homely hen lays one.
The codfish never cackles
To tell you what she'd done.
And so we scorn the codfish,
While the humble hen we prize.
Which only goes to show you
That it pays to advertise.

Anon

EGGS

Ancient civilisations ate all kinds of birds' eggs. Peacock eggs were much prized by the Romans, and ostrich eggs have been eaten since Phoenician times. Hens outrank all other eggs in popularity, with an estimated 250 billion consumed around the world each year. Duck eggs are second in commercial importance, especially in China where they are salted and preserved in lime. The eggs from geese, pheasant, turkey, quail, pigeons, guinea fowl, and gulls are eaten in different countries, if only out of curiosity.

There are also fish eggs. Caviar, the eggs of the sturgeon, is one of the most expensive gourmet delights. Lump fish and salmon's roe are the poor man's substitute. Mullet and cod provide the eggs for the Greek dish, taramasalata, a delicate pink dip made from smoked roe, oil and bread.

Sea turtle eggs from South America and Africa are another rare delicacy, much prized by connoisseurs, but their collection is restricted.

WHICH CAME FIRST, THE CHICKEN OR THE EGG?

The wild jungle fowl from Northern India seems to be the most likely ancestor of today's chicken. Men domesticated these birds around 2000 BC, but because other birds' eggs were eaten as well, the chicken didn't become popular until much later. In fact, there is no mention of eggs in the Old Testament.

Ancient Egyptians and Greeks kept chickens, and the Romans probably introduced the birds to Britain. Columbus is credited with taking the chicken to the New World, where the bird was valued more for its eggs than its flesh.

Chickens from many areas of the world have been interbred to produce famous names, such as Leghorn and Rhode Island Red. New intensive farming methods have now led to breeds of chickens which can lay large numbers of eggs in a season and even produce shell colours to suit the fashions of the day.

A chick or pullet will begin to lay eggs at 4–5 months, and can continue to produce a good supply for nearly a year. Chickens usually start laying small eggs (size 6–7), and gradually the size increases so that by the end of the egg-laying cycle they are producing large, size 1 eggs but in smaller numbers.

Each egg starts as a cell (ovum) in the reproductive system of the hen. Although the eggs we eat are unfertilised, the hen produces them at the same rate, whether the cockerel is there or not. The ovum collects the white (albumen) on its way down the oviduct, then the outside shell membrane is formed, and finally the outer shell made of calcium carbonate. Then plop! It is laid.

How do chickens lay eggs with the right thickness and colour of shell?
The colour of the egg shell depends upon the breed of the chicken. The shell thickness also varies with the breed, but depends as well upon adequate calcium in the feed and the age and health of the bird.

How can you get the right colour yolk?
People in different areas prefer different coloured yolks. Darker yolks are produced from maize-fed chickens and lighter yolks from wheat diets.

What are blood spots?
Bloodspots are harmless and occur because blood vessels near the developing egg inside the hen undergo minute rupturing.

What's inside an egg?
Crack an egg on to a white plate and take a look. On the yolk you will find the white 'germinal disc' where, in a fertilised egg, the chick would develop. At either end of the yolk is a translucent cord called the 'chalaza' which holds the yolk centrally in the white to prevent damage. Then there is the thick white, surrounded by the thin white. A membrane lines the shell, and at the blunt end is the 'air cell', which gets bigger as the egg becomes older.

EGG FARMING

There are three main systems of egg farming for the 45 million hens kept in the UK.

FREE RANGE EGGS   Over 2% of eggs are produced from free range hens who roam the land scratching for food and lay on average 140 eggs each a year. Extra food is provided and hens lay their eggs in nest boxes in hen houses. These hens need special protection at night from predators such as foxes.

Public pressure is causing the number of free range hens to increase, but figures are not yet available.

DEEP LITTER   2% of eggs are from deep litter farming. Hens are kept in large hen houses with a floor covering of deep litter – straw and wood shavings. With special feed these hens lay 250 eggs each a year. Barn eggs are a variety of deep litter production. Perches and feeders at different levels in the hen house mean that more hens can be kept in the same area.

BATTERY FARMING   96% of hens are battery farmed, although this percentage is dropping due to the demand for free range eggs. Birds are kept in cages and their diet, room temperature and lighting conditions are strictly controlled. These hens can produce 280 eggs a year.

PACKING AND STORING EGGS

Most eggs are sold to packing stations where they are tested for quality by a process called candling. Years ago, eggs were held up to a candle, but nowadays a conveyor belt passes eggs over a bright light which makes them almost transparent so faults can be detected. Eggs are sorted into three grades:

A grade eggs are perfect.

B grade eggs have slight imperfections.

C grade eggs cannot be sold to the public.

Eggs are then automatically weighed and labelled with the required EEC information. Most egg cartons are date stamped with the 'packing' and 'sell by' date (check before you buy). Eggs are graded according to weight in the size numbers 1–7. Size 3 egg is the size recommended for recipes.

Size 1: eggs weighing 70g or over.

Size 2: eggs weighing 65–70g.

Size 3: eggs weighing 60–65g.

Size 4: eggs weighing 55–60g.

Size 5: eggs weighing 50–55g.

Size 6: eggs weighing 45–50g.

Size 7: eggs weighing under 45g.

Until 1978 eggs were measured this way:

Large: $2^{3}/_{16}$ oz or more.

Standard: $1^{7}/_{8}$–$2^{3}/_{16}$ oz.

Medium: $1^{5}/_{8}$–$1^{7}/_{8}$ oz.

Small: $1^{1}/_{2}$–$1^{5}/_{8}$ oz.

TESTING FOR FRESHNESS

In the past there were no 'sell by' dates and cooks tested for themselves. Mrs Beeton recommended: 'Apply the tongue to the large end of the egg and if it feels warm, it is new.'

Wise shoppers when purchasing from primitive markets take along a bucket of water. They drop in the eggs and any bad ones will float to the top! This simple freshness test can be done at home. Put the eggs in a jug of salted water. Stale eggs with large air cells will float.

Another test is to look at a cracked egg on a plate. A fresh egg has three distinct parts – the domed yolk, a thick white and a thin white. With age the whites merge and the yolk flattens. In a really stale egg, hydrogen sulphide develops, giving off a dreadful smell.

STORING TIPS

* Store eggs at room temperature for up to two weeks, longer if kept in the fridge.
* If eggs are kept in the fridge, remove 30 minutes before cooking to bring them to room temperature.
* Egg shells are porous, so keep them away from strong smells – onions or curry.
* Store blunt end uppermost.
* If storing cracked eggs in the fridge, cover with a little water to prevent drying.

In the past, cooks used to rub butter on to egg shells to preserve the egg. This idea was not so stupid, as the butter sealed the porous shell. In the USA and Canada eggs are sprayed with oil to prevent deterioration.

Spring and summer used to bring a glut of eggs, so eggs were preserved in waterglass for up to a year. Waterglass is a solution of sodium silicate. The eggs were packed in their shells in large jars and the waterglass solution poured over and the jar stoppered. This sealed the pores of the shell, keeping bacteria out and moisture in. The eggs just needed washing before use. A great favourite during and immediately after the Second World War.

FREEZING EGGS

Cracked eggs out of their shell can be stored in the freezer for up to six months.

WHOLE EGGS Beat 4–6 eggs together, adding a little salt or sugar to prevent thickening. Pack in a plastic box, label and freeze. Individual eggs can be frozen in ice cube trays.

SEPARATED EGGS Useful for meringues and soufflés. Mix the yolks with a little salt or sugar and freeze in cartons or ice cube trays. Whites can be frozen without sugar or salt.

PICKLED EGGS

Make your own version with spices.

16–20 size 5 eggs, hardboiled and shelled
3 red or green chillies cut into strips

SPICED VINEGAR

2–2½ pints (1–1½ litres) white malt vinegar
1 inch (2cm) root ginger, peeled and cut into pieces
1 dessertspoon whole peppercorns
1 dessertspoon allspice berries

Boil the vinegar with the spices for 5 minutes. Strain into a bowl and cool.

Pack the eggs into wide necked jars with strips of chilli. Fill with enough spiced vinegar to cover the eggs. Screw or tie down and leave for 3–4 weeks before eating.

NUTRITIONAL VALUE OF EGGS

TRUE OR FALSE?

Free range eggs are more nutritious than others
False. The amounts of protein and vitamins in battery and free range eggs are nearly the same.

Brown eggs are better than white
False. Since you don't eat the shell, it doesn't matter. White eggs are increasingly difficult to find.

Darker yolks are better
False. The colour of the yolk is no indicator of the nutritional value, but more to do with the breed of chicken and what it has been fed on.

The yolk is more nutritious than the white
Truish. The protein content of white and yolk is similar, but the yolk contains less water and has more vitamins.

Eggs are indigestible
False. Eggs can be cooked in so many ways. Lightly boiled eggs have traditionally been served as 'invalid food'. The origin of this myth may have come from the fact that eggs 'bind' ingredients together, such as meatballs.

Cholesterol in eggs is bad for us
The body makes 80% of its own cholesterol and only 20% comes from food. Egg yolks, offal and some animal fats are sources of cholesterol, but if you cut down on these foods the body manufactures its own. Recent research shows that if we eat a diet high in fibre and low in fat, then eggs present no problem to the cholesterol level in the blood.

THE FACTS

Since an egg is the start of new life, it contains all the nutrients essential to life. An egg produces 11% of the daily protein requirement. Egg protein is a high quality protein since it contains all the amino acids essential for growth.

Eggs are a good source of vitamins A, B group and D, but don't provide vitamin C. Only 10% of the egg is fat, most of which is unsaturated fat, recommended for a healthy diet. The yolks contain cholesterol. The role of cholesterol in the diet is still not clear but research shows that, in conjunction with a healthy diet, if eggs are eaten the cholesterol level is not affected.

Eggs are rich in the important minerals: iron for healthy blood, and calcium for bones and teeth. They contain little carbohydrate and no dietary fibre.

Eggs are a useful food for slimmers since an average egg provides only 80 calories.

EGG RATIONING

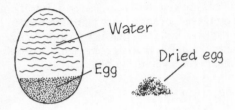

During the Second World War, eggs were rationed to ½–2 eggs per person per week, but by 1942 dried egg powder was introduced. The Ministry of Food tried to persuade people to use it with slogans such as: 'Shell eggs are five sixths water. Why import water?' To use the powder, you just mixed one part dried egg with two parts warm water and whisked away the lumps. Many remember dried egg as being rubbery, leathery, dry and tasteless.

War time recipes were inventive. Josephine Terry in a recipe called 'Eggs, none for breakfast', suggested cooking tinned apricots in bacon fat and serving them on toast. Custard powder was another egg substitute: lemon curd could be made from custard powder, citric acid and sugar – a bit like today's shop-bought versions!

EASTER EGGS

Eggs have formed part of the pagan spring festival offerings since ancient times, and the Christian Church adopted eggs as a symbol of the Resurrection. To the ancient Greeks, Chinese and Persians, the egg was a symbol of creation, of life itself. The Egyptians believed that the egg was the original cell which gave birth to the Universe and they forbade their priests to eat them in case they destroyed the origin of life itself. The Chinese, as long ago as 900 BC, exchanged red eggs at their spring festival, as did the Persians at their 'Feast of the Red Egg'.

As Christianity spread through Western Europe, pagan traditions and festivals became 'Christianised'. So the 'Feast of the Spring Equinox' became Easter. Saint Augustine is supposed to have decided that the egg should represent the resurrection of Christ, a symbol of the rolling away of the stone from the sepulchre.

Early Christians called the festival 'Paschal', after the Hebrew word for the Jewish Passover celebration at the spring equinox. The word 'Easter' derives from 'Eostre', the Anglo Saxon goddess of spring.

From the 4th century AD the church forbade eggs to be eaten during the 40–day fast of Lent. This led to a huge glut of eggs by Easter time and probably the contests and games using eggs at Easter were devised to dispose of the surplus.

Until the 17th century, only natural eggs were painted and decorated to be given as gifts at Easter. But the royal households of Europe began to exchange elaborately painted eggs made of china, porcelain and eventually precious stones.

The Easter rabbit or hare has been a European tradition for many years. In Germany, children leave a hat or basket hidden in their gardens or houses the night before Easter Sunday. If they are lucky the rabbit fills the 'nest' with brightly coloured eggs.

The first chocolate Easter eggs were made in France in the 19th century, and in Britain during the 1870s. We now spend £100 million on Easter eggs each year. The most popular are the cream-filled eggs with coloured yolks; 200 million were eaten in 1986.

FABERGÉ'S EASTER EGGS

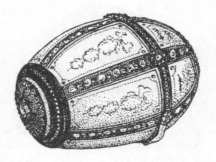

Probably the most fantastic eggs were designed by the jeweller, Carl Fabergé, for the Russian and European royal families. Tsar Alexander III commissioned the first egg in 1884 for his Empress. Inside this egg was a golden yolk which held a coloured gold hen with a diamond Imperial crown inside it. Inside the crown was a tiny ruby egg. Over a period of 30 years, 57 Imperial eggs were created.

The Queen owns two Fabergé eggs. One is made of a network of platinum set with diamonds, emeralds, sapphires and rubies. Hidden inside is the surprise, a cameo of the five Imperial children. These eggs are on display at the Queen's Gallery by Buckingham Palace.

In 1986, an Imperial Fabergé egg, presented by Tsar Nicholas II and containing a miniature clock, was sold in New York for £1 million.

COLOURED AND DECORATED EGGS

Egg colouring and decorating is an old custom. Ancient civilisations in China, Persia and Greece dyed eggs. Polish legend tells that Mary coloured eggs for Jesus to play egg rolling games, an idea which is not substantiated by the Bible.

Plant dyes were used in the past to colour eggs. Beetroot gives a pinkish red colour, spinach a yellowish green, and tea or coffee a brown colour. Choose white or very pale eggs and boil them for 30 minutes in water containing the chosen plant dye. Add vinegar to the water to give a stronger colour. Polish eggs with a little oil when they are ready.

Today, strong chemical dyes and food colourings can be used to produce vivid shell colours. These are particularly popular in Germany, Austria and Belgium where coloured eggs are found in shops and banks at Easter time. The eggs are usually hardboiled but may be blown. (To blow an egg, the egg is pierced at both ends with a needle or other sharp implement, then the contents is blown out into a dish. It needs a lot of puff!)

In many parts of the world egg decorating is an art industry:

* Polish *pysanki* eggs have patterns scratched into the coloured eggs using a sharp instrument or pen dipped in hydrochloric acid.

* Patterns are drawn on the shells using melted wax and the eggs left in a lukewarm dye bath; the wax is later removed, leaving behind a paler design on the egg shell.

* In Eastern European countries, eggs may be decorated with wool, pith from reeds and straw.

* In Holland, Germany and America, Easter trees are made from coloured branches or pieces of palm tree. The branches are hung with decorated eggs, Easter rabbits and coloured sweets, just like a Christmas tree.

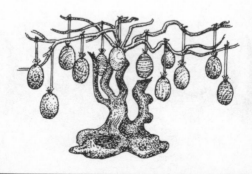

Egg Games

Egg Rolling

Generations of children have played egg rolling games at Easter time, a symbol of rolling back the stone from the sepulchre, and a way of using up all the spare eggs from the Lenten fast. In England, Preston is the only town which continues this tradition. Thousands of people bring coloured hard boiled eggs to Avenham Park on Easter Monday and roll them down the grassy slopes.

In America, in the gardens of the White House, over 10,000 eggs are rolled down the slight slope on the lawns. President Madison's wife, Dolly, started this tradition in 1877. It is the only chance the public get to walk on the White House lawns, and adults are only admitted with children.

EGG TAPPING

For this game, each player holds a hardboiled egg in their hand and the other person bangs the egg with theirs until one breaks. This game is only played in a few parts of Europe (Germany and Czechoslovakia) and is known in northern England as 'egg shackling'.

PACE EGGING

The north of England tradition of Pace egging – named after the Hebrew 'Paschal' – was a way of begging for eggs to use in Easter games. Men dressed in animal skins, blackened their faces and toured the streets carrying baskets to collect the Pace eggs. These eggs were hardboiled, coloured with plant dye then used for competitions or gifts.

EGG AND SPOON RACES

A hardboiled or raw egg (for the daring) is carried in a spoon, with the other hand kept behind the back. The runners race off and if they drop their egg they must pick it up (using the spoon only), return to the starting position, and start again. The winner is the first person over the finishing line, still carrying an egg in their spoon.

EGGS AND FOLKLORE

* Throughout history eggs have been a symbol for new life and prosperity.

* In 17th-century France, the bride smashed an egg as she entered her new home to ensure fertility.

* In Czechoslovakia, on Shrove Tuesday, a man dressed in straw would go round the village. At each home the lady would pluck off a piece of straw to put under her chickens to encourage egg laying. But did the man always wear enough straw?

* In England on New Year's Eve, and in Scotland at Hallowe'en, eggs were used to tell fortunes. An egg white was dropped into water, and from the shapes it formed fortune tellers could predict the future.

* If you dream about eggs, then the future brings riches, good luck and news of a wedding. However, if the eggs in your dreams were cracked or broken, you will shortly have a quarrel with your lover.

* The Romans placed eggs in the tombs beside their dead, and funeral caskets were often egg shaped. The link between eggs and the dead is a mystery, but eggs have been found in ancient burial grounds throughout Europe. Before that bird became extinct, the Maoris buried their dead with a moa's egg in one hand.

EGGS IN CHINA

* In China eggs are a symbol of good luck and happiness. Traditionally, at birth a child is given a red egg – a happy, lucky colour.

* Chinese thousand-year-old eggs are actually only about 100 days old. Raw duck eggs are coated in a mixture of lime, pine ash, salt and rice husks for 50–100 days to preserve them. The chemicals soak into the shell and change the egg white and yolk into a bluish green colour and the egg becomes firm. The eggs have a slightly fishy taste and are eaten with Chinese mixed pickles and soy sauce as an appetiser.

  Salted duck eggs are considered a delicacy in China. The eggs are covered with a black salted paste and left for several weeks. The paste is then removed and the eggs are gently cooked with rice and give the dish a strong flavour.

CULINARY PROPERTIES OF EGGS

As well as being nutritious, eggs play many important culinary roles.

Eggs *bind* ingredients together, such as croquettes, fish cakes and meat balls. The stickiness of the egg holds the pieces of food together until, on heating, the egg protein coagulates and sets, and the mixture becomes firm.

Eggs are used to *glaze* pastries and buns. Beaten egg, sometimes diluted with milk, is brushed over the surface and cooks to a glossy, golden brown finish.

When beaten, whole eggs, egg yolks and whites are *capable of holding air*, and so help lighten mixtures such as soufflés, meringues, sponges and choux pastry. When whole eggs are whisked, the egg protein molecules uncoil (denature) and surround and trap globules of air, forming a foam. This foam is the basis of sponge cake mixtures. On cooking, the air expands and the egg and flour proteins set, to produce a light, airy cake.

Egg yolks can be whisked with sugar or fruit juice to form the basis of cold soufflés. Maximum volume is obtained when yolks are whisked over steam heat.

As egg whites are whisked, the albumen (the egg white protein) extends and incorporates air forming a foam. Merginues made from whisked egg white and sugar dry out on heating, the air expands and the albumen coagulates, forming a fine honeycomb structure.

Eggs, especially the yolks, contain an *emulsifying agent* which is able to hold together liquids, such as oil and water, and stop them separating. Egg yolk, with its emulsifying agent, holds together oil and vinegar for mayonnaise, and butter in suspension for Hollandaise sauce.

Eggs form a *coating* outside foods and can hold a further coating, such as breadcrumbs, to the food. When the food if fried, the egg coagulates and forms a seal to protect the food inside from the fat.

Eggs are used to *thicken* sauces such as custards. With gentle heat, the egg protein coagulates and thickens the sauce. Overheating causes overcoagulation of the egg protein and syneresis (weeping out of liquid) and the sauce separates and curdles.

Crushed egg shell and egg white are *clarifying agents* when whisked into hot jellies. They absorb unwanted food particles and then are strained off to leave a clear jelly.

In cakes, batters and pastries, eggs help *form the structure*. The proteins in the eggs, flour and other ingredients coagulate and set on heating.

Eggs *hinder sugar crystallisation* in confectionary and freezing. When egg whites are added to a sorbet, they stabilise the frozen mixture and hinder the growth of ice crystals.

Hard boiled eggs may be used to *garnish* slices. Finely chopped whites and sieved yolks (mimosa) are a traditional garnish for dressed crab. Strips of omelette decorate rice dishes in the Far East.

COOKING WITH EGGS

WHAT WENT WRONG?

Mistakes can occur when cooking with eggs. It helps to know *why* something has gone wrong as well as *how* to save a dish from disaster.

Why does mayonnaise sometimes separate?
If the oil is added too quickly the mixture curdles. Start with a fresh egg and add the curdled mixture to it. Eggs should be at room temperature for best results.

Why won't my egg whites whisk up easily?
Fat interferes with the egg white foam, so any yolk or fat left in the mixing bowl or on the equipment used will spoil the result. Crack each egg into a cup first in case you make a mistake when separating, and use fresh eggs at room temperature. Grease sticks to plastic bowls very easily so avoid them when whisking egg whites, just in case.

Why do hardboiled egg yolks turn black?
The iron in the yolk combines with the sulphur in the egg white to form the greyish black iron sulphide. To avoid this, don't overcook the eggs, and cool hardboiled eggs quickly in cold water.

How can I make smooth egg custards?
If a baked egg custard is cooked at too high a temperature for too long, the egg protein coagulates and shrinks, forming holes. Liquid seeps out and the texture of the custard is spoiled. Bake the custard in a bain marie to protect it from fierce heat.

Why do egg shells crack during boiling?
Eggs taken straight from the fridge are too cold to cook in boiling water and the 'thermal shock' causes them to crack, so use eggs at room temperature or run some warm water over them first. Vigorous boiling cracks the eggs as they bang together during cooking. Eggs also crack when put in cold water because air trapped within the egg expands as the egg heats up. Sometimes the air is expelled through the porous shell; sometimes not. Pressure builds up and the egg cracks. Prick a hole in the blunt end of the shell (where the air sac lies) and you'll see a jet of air expelled as the water heats up. Use the pin-hole trick when you put them in boiling water too.

Why do my soufflés sometimes collapse?
If you take a soufflé out of the oven too long before it is eaten, it will collapse. The hot air cools down and escapes, so the mixture sinks. To avoid this, once the soufflé is cooked, hold it in a low oven until needed – and tell your guests to be prompt!

Why do my eggs taste of onions?
Incorrect storage. Egg shells are porous and absorb strong smells.

MAKING CRISP MERINGUES

There are several reasons why meringues can go wrong:

1. If egg whites are only whisked to the 'softly stiff' stage when the sugar is added, they take much longer to whisk up again to make a stiff meringue.

2. If the egg whites are whisked for too long, they become too dry when the sugar is added. On heating, the egg white collapses, releasing sugar droplets on to the surface.

3. If granulated sugar is used instead of caster sugar, the sharp crystals break down the foam and the meringue collapses.

4. If the sugar is added too quickly and then not whisked in properly, the result is a sticky, chewy meringue.

5. Finally, meringues need to be baked in a low oven for at least an hour. Softer meringues, which are cooked at higher temperatures should be eaten at once, otherwise they collapse.

Aren't meringues complicated?

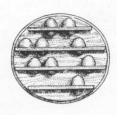

So You Can't Even Boil An Egg?

There is an art to boiling an egg. Here are some tips.
* Eggs taken straight from the fridge crack easily when immersed in boiling water. Use eggs at room temperature, or else cook in cold water and bring slowly to the boil. Prick the blunt end first to release pressure build up.
* Boil eggs gently for 3½–4 minutes for *lightly boiled* eggs. Smaller eggs take less time to cook. *Hardboiled* eggs take 10–12 minutes to cook.
* Boiled eggs are usually eaten hot. Hard boiled eggs should be plunged into cold water to prevent a dark ring forming.

SCRAMBLED EGGS   Use 2 eggs per person and beat the eggs with 1 tablespoon milk, salt and pepper. Melt 1 oz (25g) butter in a pan, pour in the eggs and cook over a gentle heat, stirring occasionally until the mixture is creamy and thick. Serve at once.

MICROWAVE SCRAMBLED EGGS   Using the recipe above, melt the butter in a bowl in a microwave. Add the eggs and cook for 1 minute, then stir, replace in the oven and cook for a further 2–3 minutes until the mixture is thick.

FRIED EGGS   Heat a little oil in a frying pan. Break in the eggs, one at a time, and cook until the white is set and firm but the yolk still runny. The Americans call this egg 'sunny side up'. If the fried egg is flipped over to cook the top side then you have made a 'right side over easy'.

MICROWAVE FRIED AND POACHED EGGS   Prick the yolk gently a couple of times with a cocktail stick before cooking to prevent the egg from exploding. Cover loosely with clingfilm after placing either in oil, for fried egg, or water for poached egg. Cook for 1–1½ minutes and leave to stand for 1–2 minutes.

POACHED EGGS   In Britain eggs are often cooked in special cups in an egg poacher. These eggs should really be called 'steamed eggs' as real poached eggs are cooked in simmering salted water.

Crack the eggs in a cup, then slide them into simmering salted water and poach for 2–3 minutes. Remove with a slotted spoon and drain off excess water before serving on hot buttered toast or (for a main meal) with potatoes and a cheesy sauce.

BAKED EGGS   Crack an egg into a greased ramekin dish and cover with salt, pepper, and a little milk and a knob of butter. Bake in a moderate oven 350°F/180°C/Gas 4 for 8–10 minutes until the white begins to set. The topping may be varied – try grated cheese, chopped chives or tomato juice.

BASIC OMELETTE

The perfect omelette is golden and light. In France, where it originates, the centre of the omelette is served semi liquid or creamy. Omelettes may be plain or filled with a savoury or sweet filling.

1/2 oz (15g) butter
3 eggs, size 3
3 teaspoons water
salt and pepper
filling of your choice: herbs, grated cheese, sautéed sliced
  mushrooms, chopped ham, etc.

Gently melt the butter in a 7–8 inch (18–20cm) non-stick omelette pan.

Beat the eggs, water and seasoning together until fluffy. Pour the egg mixture into the pan, and using a wooden spoon or spatula, draw the mixture from the edge of the pan to the middle to cook the runny egg. When firm and golden underneath, and soft and slightly runny on top, add the filling, if used, then fold the omelette in half or serve flat.

Serves 1

EGG RECIPES

MAYONNAISE

Some say that mayonnaise was invented by the chef of the Duc de Richelieu in 1756 to celebrate the capture of Port Mahon in Minorca. More likely it comes from the old French word for 'egg yolk' – 'moyen', and so 'moyennaise'.

1 whole egg or 2 egg yolks
pinch each of caster sugar, dried mustard, salt and pepper
¼ pint (150ml) vegetable oil
1 tablespoon wine vinegar or lemon juice

Beat together the egg, sugar, mustard, salt and pepper in a bowl. Very slowly add the oil, drop by drop at first, beating all the time. As the mixture thickens the oil can be added more quickly. Finally stir in the vinegar or lemon juice and adjust the seasoning.

   *For speed, whizz up the mayonnaise in a blender or food processor, taking care to add the oil slowly at first.

Mayonnaise with fresh herbs and yoghurt
Mix natural yoghurt, some freshly chopped parsley
and a clove of crushed garlic into the mayonnaise.
Serve with baked potatoes, salad or fish.

Mayonnaise Marie Rose
Mix a little tomato purée, Tabasco sauce and natural
yoghurt into the mayonnaise and serve with seafood
salads.

HOLLANDAISE SAUCE

By using a blender, this sauce, which is quite difficult to make by hand, becomes very easy!

2 eggs
1 tablespoon fresh lemon juice
salt and freshly ground black pepper
4 oz (100g) melted butter

Whizz the eggs, lemon juice and seasoning in a
blender and slowly pour in a stream of melted
butter. Season to taste. Either use the sauce at once,
or keep warm over a saucepan of simmering water.
    Serve with grilled salmon steaks, trout, asparagus
or broccoli.

Avgolemono Soup

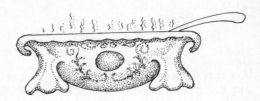

This famous Greek soup is flavoured with lemon juice and thickened with eggs.

2 oz (50g) short grain rice
1¾ pints (about 1 litre) good chicken stock
2 eggs
juice of a lemon

Boil the rice in the chicken stock until tender. Cool slightly. Beat together the eggs and lemon juice and add a little stock. Add a little more stock and stir well then slowly pour this mixture back into the soup and heat gently but do not boil. Serve immediately.

Serves 4–6

HUEVOS RANCHEROS
(RANCHERS EGGS)

A Mexican breakfast dish of fried eggs spiced with
hot chillies. This will wake you up!

Sauce
1 small onion, finely chopped
1 clove garlic, crushed
2 tablespoons oil
1 small can tomatoes, drained and chopped
1–2 green chillies, deseeded and finely chopped
salt and black pepper

6 tortillas or pitta bread
oil for frying
6 eggs
1 large avocado, sliced thinly

Fry the onion and garlic in the oil until soft then add
the tomatoes, chillies, salt and pepper. Stir then
cover and cook for 15 minutes.

Warm the tortillas or pitta bread under the grill.
Heat the oil in a large frying pan and fry all the eggs
together until the whites are firm and the yolks soft.
Separate each egg and serve on a tortilla or pitta
bread. Spoon on some hot sauce and garnish with
slices of avocado.

Serves 4–6

SPICED EGG SANDWICH

Cook the eggs in a microwave or a saucepan for this speedy snack. This spiced egg sandwich is very useful for picnics and packed lunches. Decorate with salad ingredients.

4 wholemeal baps
4 beaten eggs
1 tablespoon tomato purée
several dashes Tabasco sauce to taste
½ avocado, peeled and diced
½ red pepper, finely diced

Split the baps in half and grill.

Mix together the remaining ingredients. Cook the egg mixture either in the microwave oven, stirring once during cooking, until the mixture is softly firm. Or heat a little butter in a pan and cook over a gentle heat until the egg scrambles. Serve piled on top of each halved bap, garnished with a little salad.

Serves 4

TORTILLA

This crisp Spanish omelette, traditionally made from potatoes, onions and eggs, can be served hot or cold. In Spanish bars, slices of tortilla are served as *tapas*, tasty snacks to be eaten with drinks.

1 lb (450g) potatoes, peeled and diced
1 medium onion, finely chopped
3 tablespoons oil (olive oil is traditionally used)
salt and black pepper
6 eggs

Fry the potatoes and onion in 2 tablespoons oil in a non-stick omelette pan, 8 inches (20cm) in diameter. Stir occasionally and cook for 20 minutes with a lid on until soft and slightly browned. Season with salt and pepper. Remove and wipe out the pan.

Beat the eggs and stir in the potato mixture. Add the remaining oil to the pan, heat, then add the egg mixture. Cook for 2–3 minutes until the base of the omelette is firm. Grill the top of the omelette for 3–4 minutes until golden and softly firm. Slide the tortilla out on to a plate and cut into portions. Serve warm.

Serves 4–6

SALADE NIÇOISE

A hors d'oeuvre from the South of France. Add tuna fish and cooked french beans to make an excellent summer lunch, or use as a filling for large rolls.

a crisp lettuce, shredded into chunks
2–3 hardboiled eggs cut in quarters, lengthways
2 tomatoes, quartered
1 small can anchovy fillets, drained
10–12 black olives
French dressing

Arrange the lettuce, eggs, tomatoes, anchovy fillets and olives in a bowl. Just before serving, pour the dressing over the salad.

PIPERADE

This Basque speciality, an open omelette topped with onions, peppers and tomatoes, is delicious served as a snack, starter or main course.

oil for frying
1 onion, finely sliced
2 red or green peppers, deseeded and cut into strips
1 clove garlic, crushed
pinch dried basil
salt and black pepper
1 small can tomatoes, drained and tomatoes chopped
4 beaten eggs

Fry the onion in 2 tablespoons of oil until soft, then stir in the peppers. Cover and cook for 15 minutes. Add the garlic, basil, salt and pepper and tomatoes and cook a further 5 minutes with the lid off.

Heat 1 tablespoon oil in a non-stick omelette pan and pour in the beaten eggs. Stir until the eggs begin to set, then cover with the pepper mixture, mixing it gently into the eggs. Serve in wedges.

Southern Indian Egg Curry

These hardboiled eggs are served in a spicy sauce made with coconut milk.

2 onions, finely chopped
2 cloves garlic, crushed
2 tablespoons oil
2 tablespoons curry paste (adjust to taste)
2 tablespoons tomato purée
1/2 pint (300ml) coconut milk (see packet instructions)
8–12 hardboiled eggs

Fry the onions and garlic in the oil until soft. Stir in the curry paste and tomato purée, then pour in the coconut milk. Bring to the boil and simmer gently to make a thick sauce. Place the hardboiled eggs in the sauce and cook for a further 5 minutes so that the eggs are flavoured by the sauce. Serve hot with boiled rice and chutney.

Serves 4–6

KOOKOO SABZI
(LEEK AND HERB OMELETTE)

Savoury omelettes are eaten throughout the Middle East and are cut into wedges and eaten as snacks or main meals. In Iran this thick omelette is served with yoghurt.

3 tablespoons oil
1 lb (450g) leeks, washed and finely diced
4 spring onions, finely chopped
2 oz (50g) finely chopped parsley
1 tablespoon dried or freshly chopped dill
1 clove garlic, crushed
6 eggs
salt and black pepper

Heat 2 tablespoons oil in a 8 inch (20cm) non-stick omelette pan and fry the leeks, spring onions, parsley, dill and garlic for 5 minutes until soft. Remove and wipe out the pan.

Mix the vegetables with the beaten eggs and season well. Heat the remaining oil and pour in the egg mixture. Cook on a very low heat for 20 minutes until the base is golden brown. Grill the top of the omelette for a few minutes until lightly browned.

Serve hot or cold, cut into wedges with salad and yoghurt.

Serves 4–6

EGG FRIED RICE

This is a favourite dish of Chinese restaurants. Left-over cooked rice can be quickly stir fried with all kinds of ingredients to make a meal.

4 tablespoons oil
3 beaten eggs
1 clove garlic, crushed
1 inch (2cm) fresh ginger, peeled and chopped
2 carrots, peeled and cut into strips
3–4 spring onions, shredded into strips
7 oz (200g) cooked prawns
1 medium can sweetcorn, drained
1 lb (450g) cooked rice
soy sauce

Heat 2 tablespoons oil in a wok or large saucepan. Pour in the egg, then stir quickly to make a soft, scrambled egg. Remove the egg and put on one side. Wipe out the wok or pan.

Heat the remaining oil and stir fry the garlic, ginger and strips of carrot for 1–2 minutes. Add the spring onions, prawns and sweetcorn and cook for 3–4 minutes, then add the rice. Toss and stir vigorously until the mixture is hot. Season with soy sauce, then stir in the cooked egg. Serve hot.

Serves 4–6

EGG FOO YUNG

Serve as one large pancake or several small ones.

oil for frying
3–4 mushrooms, cut into slivers
3–4 spring onions cut into shreds
4 oz (100g) cooked shelled prawns
4 oz (100g) beansprouts
3 eggs

SAUCE
1/2 pint (300ml) chicken stock
3 teaspoons soy sauce
2 teaspoons cornflour mixed with a little water

Heat 2 tablespoons oil in a wok or large frying pan and stir fry the mushrooms, spring onions and prawns for 1–2 minutes. Add the beansprouts for 30 seconds, then remove from the heat. Beat the eggs in a bowl and stir in the cooked mixture.

Wipe out the wok with a paper towel. Add a little more oil and heat. Pour in 2 tablespoonfuls of egg mixture and leave to cook until firm. Turn the pancake over and cook until golden. Remove and keep warm. Make the remaining mixture into 6–8 pancakes, adding more oil if necessary.

For the sauce, heat all the ingredients together in a pan and stir until thick and clear. Serve the egg foo yung hot with boiled rice and sauce.

Serves 4

PINEAPPLE AND KIWI FRUIT PAVLOVA

A soft centred meringue recipe, supposedly created for the Russian ballerina Anna Pavlova when she toured Australia.

3 egg whites
1 level teaspoon cornflour
1 teaspoon vinegar
1 teaspoon vanilla essence
7 oz (200g) caster sugar
1/4 pint (150ml) whipping cream
fresh pineapple chunks
2 kiwi fruit, peeled and sliced

Set the oven at 300°F/150°C/Gas 2. Cover a baking sheet with non-stick paper and draw on an 8 inch (20cm) circle.

In a clean bowl whisk the egg whites until stiff but not dry. Mix in the cornflour, vinegar and vanilla essence, then gradually beat in the sugar. Continue beating for several minutes to make a heavy, smooth mixture.

Spread the meringue over the paper and bake for 1 hour, until the meringue is crisp and firm on the outside with a marshmallow texture inside. Allow to cool in the oven.

Whip the cream and fill the pavlova with cream, chunks of pineapple and slices of kiwi fruit.

Serves 4–6

FLAN
(CARAMEL CUSTARD)

In Spanish-speaking countries, 'flan' is a favourite dessert, but the recipe is the same as our caramel custard.

4 oz (100g) granulated sugar
6 eggs
¾ pint (450ml) milk
3 oz (75g) caster sugar

Heat the granulated sugar in a heavy-based saucepan until golden brown. Pour this caramel into 6 moulds or an ovenproof dish and place in a bain marie (a roasting tin half filled with water).

Beat together the eggs, milk and caster sugar and strain the mixture on to the caramel. Bake in a moderate oven, 350°F/180°C/Gas 4 for 20–25 minutes or longer, until the custard is firm. Chill before serving and then turn the custard out on to a dish.

Serves 4–6

SAINT CLEMENT'S SOUFFLE

This pudding got its name from the nursery rhyme, since oranges and lemons are the main ingredients.

5 eggs, separated
5 oz (150g) caster sugar
1 oz (25g) cornflour
½ pint (300ml) milk
4 fl oz (100ml) orange juice
juice and rind of a lemon

Cream together the egg yolks and caster sugar. Stir in the cornflour, then mix in the milk. Heat very gently until the mixture thickens, cool slightly then add the orange and lemon juice and lemon rind.

Whisk the egg whites until stiff, then fold a tablespoon into the orange mixture. Carefully fold in the remaining egg white. Pour into a greased ovenproof dish and bake at 375°F/190°C/Gas 5 for 30–35 minutes until well risen and golden. Eat immediately.

Serves 4–6

CHOCOLATE MOUSSE

This is probably the most popular dessert in France, and such a simple recipe.

7 oz (200g) dark chocolate
4 eggs, separated

Melt the chocolate in a bowl over a pan of hot water, or in a microwave oven. (Take care not to get water in the chocolate.) Stir in the egg yolks.

Whisk the egg whites until stiff but not dry. Fold a little egg white into the chocolate, then gradually fold in the rest. Spoon into 4 glasses and leave to set.

Serves 4

VERMOUTH ZABAGLIONE

Traditionally zabaglione is made with Marsala, but vermouth makes an excellent substitute.

4 egg yolks and one whole egg
2 oz (50g) caster sugar
1/2 wine glass vermouth – red or white
4 sponge fingers

Beat together the eggs and sugar in a bowl over a saucepan of boiling water. Whisk for 5–7 minutes until the eggs are creamy and fluffy. Gradually add the vermouth and continue whisking until thick. Spoon into serving glasses and decorate with sponge fingers. Serve warm.

Serves 4

COOKING WITH OTHER BIRDS' EGGS

DUCK EGGS

Duck eggs are larger, richer and taste slightly oilier than hens' eggs. They must be eaten fresh as the eggs are often laid in muddy areas and can become contaminated with salmonella bacteria, which cause food poisoning. Duck eggs should be thoroughly cooked by boiling for 15 minutes or used for baked cakes or custards.

GOOSE EGGS

Goose eggs are larger than duck eggs and more expensive. They taste quite oily and should be served very fresh in briefly cooked dishes.

PHEASANT OR PARTRIDGE EGGS

These little eggs often have white, buff or speckled shells. They are not widely available, although they can be bought from pheasant farms. They are usually served hard-boiled, pickled or set in aspic.

QUAILS' EGGS

These tiny eggs are considered a great delicacy and can be eaten soft or hard boiled, poached or set in aspic.

QUAILS' EGGS AND BACON SALAD

A dainty colourful starter for a special occasion. If quails' eggs are difficult to find, use four hens' eggs instead.

few leaves of radicchio
some curly endive
bunch of watercress, washed, trimmed and chopped
16–20 quails' eggs
7 oz (200 g) smoked bacon, cut into dice
juice of ½ lemon
2 tablespoons olive oil
1 tablespoon wine vinegar
salt and black pepper
chopped chives for garnish

Mix together the radicchio, endive and watercress in a large salad bowl.

Heat ½ pint (300 ml) water and the lemon juice in a large frying pan. Break the quails' eggs on to a plate. When the water bubbles, slide the eggs carefully into the pan. Poach gently for 1 minute, then remove and keep warm.

Fry the bacon in a frying pan until crisp and brown. Drain on kitchen paper. Mix together the oil, vinegar and seasoning, then toss into the salad. Stir in the pieces of bacon and lay the quails' eggs gently on top. Sprinkle with chopped chives and serve.

Serves 4

EGG DRINKS

OLD-FASHIONED EGG NOG

Nog is an Old English word for ale, and egg nog is descended from a hot drink made from ale or dry Spanish wine. Traditionally egg nog is served at Christmas.

1 egg
1 teaspoon sugar
1 measure (1 fl oz/25ml) brandy
1 measure (1 fl oz/25ml) dark rum
3 fl oz (75ml) milk
nutmeg, to decorate

Use a cocktail shaker or jam jar with a screw top lid and shake all the ingredients together vigorously. Pour into a glass and sprinkle over a little grated nutmeg.

RAMOS GIN FIZZ

A frothy, fragrant alcoholic drink, invented by Henry Ramos in New Orleans. During the Mardi Gras festivities of 1915, he employed 35 boys in his bar just to shake up Ramos Fizz for his customers.

1 dessertspoon caster sugar
juice of ½ lemon and ½ lime
3–4 dashes orange flower water
1½ measures (1½ fl oz/45ml) dry gin
1 egg white
2–3 tablespoons cream or milk
crushed ice
soda water

Pour all the ingredients except the soda water into a
cocktail shaker and shake vigorously for several
minutes until the mixture thickens. Strain into a tall
glass and top up with soda water.

TROPICAL SURPRISE

A delicious, foamy non alcoholic cocktail.

1 banana
1 egg
½ pint (300ml) orange juice
2 teaspoons honey
slices of orange to garnish

Put all the ingredients into a liquidiser and whisk
until foamy. Serve in glasses decorated with a slice of
orange.

EGGS FOR BEAUTY

DRY SKIN FACE MASK

Ingredients: 1 egg yolk
1 teaspoon of honey
1 teaspoon of fine oatmeal

To use: Mix together and spread over the face. Relax for 10 minutes, then gently wash off with warm water. Splash the face with cold water and dry with a soft towel. The oils from the egg yolk soften the skin.

OILY SKIN FACE MASK

Ingredients: a little lemon juice
1 egg white

To use: Beat together until the mixture becomes foamy. Smooth over the face and leave for 10 minutes, then gently wash off using warm water. Pat the face dry with a soft towel. The egg white and lemon help to cleanse the skin's surface.

EGGS FOR SHINY HAIR

Wash and rinse the hair then work in a beaten egg using your fingertips. Comb the mixture through the hair, then leave for 10–15 minutes before rinsing thoroughly in cool water. Do not make the water too hot or you will scramble the egg!

AN OLD RECIPE FOR HAND CREAM

'Take sweet almond, half a pound; white wine vinegar, brandy and spring water, crumb of bread and the yolks of two eggs. Blanch and beat the almonds, moistening them with the vinegar; add the crumb of bread soaked in the brandy and mix it with the almonds and yolks of egg, by repeated tirturation. Then pour in the water, and simmer the whole over a slow fire, till it has acquired a proper consistence.'

The Toilet of Flora, 1784

OTHER USES FOR EGGS

Eggs play an important part in clarifying good wine. When wine is aged in barrels, it must be 'fined' to make sure it is clear. Egg whites can be used for this as the albumen coagulates and attracts any minute particles which may be floating in the wine. The mass finally settles on the bottom of the cask. In modern wine plants today, wine is usually filtered instead of being fined.

Egg shells have their uses too. Some gardeners dig egg shells into clay soils to help improve the drainage. And people who keep hens sometimes mix crushed shells with the hen feed to improve the calcium in their diet and ensure hard eggshells.

You can use egg shells as plant pots. Dampen some cotton wool and put it inside the empty shells. Sprinkle in some seeds, and water as they grow. Cardboard egg boxes make good flower pots too, and can be used like peat pots for sprouting small seedlings.

Eggshell paint is not, in fact, made from shells but is the name of the glaze. It is between a matt and glossy finish. In 1925, *Arts and Decoration* magazine recorded 'The eggshell finish of a freshly laid egg is the dull finish decorators now prefer.'

TRICKS WITH EGGS

THE FLOATING EGG TRICK

Why does one egg float in water and the other sink?

You need: 2 large glasses, 2 eggs, and some salt. Fill the first glass with water. Fill the second glass with water, then stir in 4 tablespoons salt. See if the egg floats in this glass. If not, add more salt.

Now for the trick. Place an egg in the first glass and watch it sink (unless the egg is stale!). Do the same for the second glass, cast your spell and the egg rises! Swop your eggs over just to show your audience that the eggs are identical.

THE SPINNING EGG

This trick is fun and also useful. If you keep hardboiled eggs in the fridge this is one way to tell them apart.

You need: several raw eggs, one hardboiled egg, a plate.

Spin your hardboiled egg like a top on the plate. Now offer the raw eggs to your audience and challenge them to do the same.

The hardboiled egg is the only egg to spin. The contents of the raw egg are liquid and cannot follow the rapid spinning motion, so wobble about and cause the egg to fall over.

BOOMERANG EGGS

If you roll an egg gently on a large flat surface it will return to you. Choose pointed eggs for best results.

You need: several pointed eggs.

Gently roll the egg by pushing it with your finger. The egg should travel round them come back to you. Nature's way perhaps of returning an egg to the nest.

CAN YOU BREAK AN EGG?

This trick requires practice and you may break a few eggs along the way!

You need: several hardboiled eggs.

Hold the egg with the pointed end in the palm of one hand and the blunt end in the palm of your other hand. Now try to crush the egg. If it is held centrally, no amount of force will crush the egg. Egg sandwiches!

DID YOU KNOW. . . ?

What bird laid the largest egg?
The elephant bird, now extinct, laid eggs weighing 27lb (12.2kg), equivalent to 180 hens' eggs. The ostrich is the living bird which lays the largest eggs – on average 3½lb (1½kg), equivalent to 24 hens' eggs. Ostrich eggs take 40 minutes to boil.

The biggest hen's egg weighed 1lb (450g) and had a double yolk and double shell. Double yolkers occur when two yolks get trapped in the same shell. But what do you call the nine-yolked egg produced by an American hen in 1971?

In the past, eggs were forbidden during the 40 days' fast of Lent. Cooks beat up any spare eggs and made them into pancakes on Shrove Tuesday, the day before Lent. This gave the day its name – Pancake day. By Easter time there were so many spare eggs that games and feasts were organised to use them up.

The largest pancake was fried in Britain – at the Queen's Head Hotel in Cheltenham – in 1987. It measured 25 feet in diameter and used 5,274 eggs, 5,161 lb (2,322 kg) of flour and 92 gallons (442 litres) of milk.

The first British chocolate Easter egg was made by Fry's of Bristol in 1875. The largest chocolate egg was made in Leicester in 1982 and weighed a calorie laden 7,561lb (3,430kg).

The Americans organised the greatest egg hunt ever for 72,000 hardboiled eggs and 40,000 sugar eggs in 1985. Previously they had set the record of 4 hours 34 minutes for the longest egg and spoon race (28½ miles) and owned the record-laying chicken who laid 371 eggs in 364 days.

Did you know that you should always make a hole in an empty egg shell? Why? Witches could steal the shell, and use it as a boat to go out to sea and whip up a storm.

How far can you throw an egg without breaking it? The Finns hold the record set in 1982 of 96.90 metres (317 feet).

The most expensive eggs in the world cost £600 a kilo. They come from the Caspian sturgeon and are called Beluga Caviar.

Legend says that the ravens in the Tower of London prevent the downfall of the Tower and the country. Each week they are fed a raw egg, and they are particularly fond of the fried eggs thrown out from the guardroom.

Nearly 250 billion eggs are eaten every year around the world. The Japanese, Germans and Spanish eat the most, averaging 5½ eggs each a week. They are closely followed by the Americans, French and Austrians who eat five, with the British trailing on just under four.

The aubergine is called eggplant in some parts of the world because the plant was first named after the white variety of aubergine which has fruit the size, colour and shape of an egg.

Do you know why the egg mushroom is called Amanita Caesarea? The Caesar in question was the Emperor Claudius who was so fond of these mushrooms that he didn't notice when his wife slipped in a poisonous variety!

EGGSPRESSIONS

People have been called 'bad eggs', 'good eggs', 'old eggs' and, if they are clever enough, 'egg heads'.

Writers are fond of such expressions. Aesop began it all with 'Don't count your chickens before they are hatched.' Shakespeare countered with, '[it's] not worth an egg'. Samuel Butler pondered, 'A hen is only an egg's way of making another egg,' and then came up with his famous quote, 'Don't venture all your eggs in one basket.' Mark Twain in more modern times retaliated with 'Put all your eggs in the one basket – AND WATCH THAT BASKET.'

Robespierre, who was obviously fond of cooking, wrote, 'You can't make an omelette without breaking eggs.' Which, as sure as eggs is eggs, is teaching your grandmother to suck them!

ACKNOWLEDGEMENTS

Thanks to:
The British Egg Information Service
Preston Reference Library
Dell Foods, Berkshire
American Embassy
Sothebys

There was an old man of Madrid
Who ate sixty-five eggs for a quid.
When they asked 'Are you faint?',
He replied 'No, I ain't
But I don't feel as well as I did'.

Anon

OTHER TITLES IN THE SERIES

The Little Green Avocado Book
The Little Garlic Book
The Little Pepper Book
The Little Lemon Book
The Little Apple Book
The Little Strawberry Book
The Little Mustard Book
The Little Honey Book
The Little Nut Book
The Little Mushroom Book
The Little Bean Book
The Little Rice Book
The Little Tea Book
The Little Coffee Book
The Little Chocolate Book
The Little Curry Book
The Little Mediterranean Food Book
The Little Exotic Vegetable Book
The Little Exotic Fruit Book
The Little Yoghurt Book
The Little Tofu Book
The Little Breakfast Book
The Little Potato Book

Aquarium Fish

The illustrated identifier to over 100 freshwater species

Aquarium Fish

The illustrated identifier to over 100 freshwater species

Derek J. Lambert

APPLE

A QUINTET BOOK

Published by The Apple Press
6 Blundell Street
London N7 9BH

ISBN 1-85076-831-5

This book was designed and produced by
Quintet Publishing Limited
6 Blundell Street
London N7 9BH

Creative Director: Richard Dewing
Art Director: Silke Braun
Designer: James Lawrence
Project Editor: Diana Steedman
Editor: John Wright

Typeset in Great Britain by
Central Southern Typesetters, Eastbourne
Manufactured in Singapore by
Bright Arts (Singapore) Pte Ltd.
Printed in Singapore by
Star Standard Industries (Pte) Ltd.

CONTENTS

INTRODUCTION....................6

HOW TO USE THIS BOOK.........13

CARP-LIKE FISH 14

CATFISH 28

CHARACINS 35

CICHLIDS 42

GOBIES AND RELATED FISH 50

GOURAMIS AND OTHER
    LABYRINTH FISH 52

HALFBEAKS 57

PERCHES 59

TOOTHCARPS – EGGLAYING 62

TOOTHCARPS – LIVEBEARING 67

RAINBOW FISH AND
    SILVERSIDES 74

OTHER BONY FISHES 77

INDEX 80

INTRODUCTION

The hobby of aquarium fish-keeping has a long history, probably stretching back over 300 years. Originally only native species were kept, but there are reports of goldfish (*Carassius auratus*) reaching Europe as early as 1611 and the first tropical species, the paradise fish – (*Macropodus opercularis*) arrived in 1869. Ornamental fish-keeping and breeding, however, started long before this. In ancient Chinese records, there are reports of colored goldfish having been found as early as A.D. 265 and that serious breeding began about A.D. 800. Poetry of this period even mentions the goldfish, so they must have been widespread and popular at this time.

ABOVE: *The Paradise Fish* (Macropodus opercularis) *was the first tropical fish to be introduced to the hobby in 1869. Undoubtedly its* **tolerance** *to low temperatures helped it survive the rudimentary conditions.*

A PURELY DIAGRAMMATIC FISH TO SHOW THE POSITION OF VARIOUS FINS AND BODY PARTS

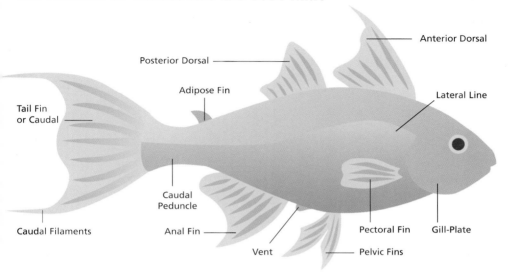

Anterior Dorsal

Posterior Dorsal

Adipose Fin

Lateral Line

Tail Fin or Caudal

Caudal Peduncle

Caudal Filaments

Anal Fin

Vent

Pelvic Fins

Pectoral Fin

Gill-Plate

WHAT IS A FISH?

A fish can be defined as any cold-blooded, legless, aquatic organism which possesses a backbone, gills, and at least a median fin as well as a tail. Of the animals which this definition includes, two classes compose what most people think of as fish. These are Chrondrichthyes (sharks and rays), which have a cartilaginous skeleton, and Osteichthyes, which are the bony fish. Despite both these classes also having well-developed gill arches, a pair of pectoral fins, and a pair of pelvic fins, some scientists say only the bony fish should be considered as true fish.

Even if you only include the bony fish, there are over 25,000 species of fish in the world that have adapted to live in almost every aquatic habitat, from the deepest oceans to the shallowest streams. You can even find fish in the most unlikely of habitats. In underground rivers, they have adapted to life without light and survive on only the most minimal amounts of food. In ponds and rivers which dry up during the dry season, the fish have to dig themselves a burrow in the mud and hibernate for many months or lay eggs in the substrate which hatch out when the rains come.

MOVING AROUND

Fish move in a variety of ways and use each fin in a very specific way to generate motion. The most common method is to move the caudal fin from side to side to generate forward motion, but this is more often used when the fish wants a sudden burst of speed or is fighting against a current. The rest of the time, the pectoral fins are often employed. These much smaller fins are positioned on each side of the body behind the gill plates and move the fish around in a much more gentle fashion using less energy than the caudal fin.

Some fish have unusual body shapes or fins and employ different methods to move around. Knifefish have a small or thread-like dorsal fin, but the anal fin is extended along almost the whole length of the body. This undulates in a similar way to a snake and produces forward or backward motion as the fish desires. Mudskippers have developed very strong pectoral fins which enable them to hold their body up and "walk" over land. Other fish will jump clear out of the water to reach flying insects or escape danger, and some will even haul themselves out of a pond or river and then slither like a snake through the damp grass to reach a different habitat. Several predatory fish find this a very useful talent!

DIETARY REQUIREMENTS

It would be very easy if all fish ate the same diet and all we aquarists had to do was put a pinch of flake food in the tank a couple of times a day. The fact is that every species of fish has evolved in a specific way to eat certain types of food. Some feed primarily on vegetable matter while others are predators which eat only live foods, such as insects or fish. There are even specialist feeders which eat only the scales or eyes of other fish.

While such specialist feeders are not generally kept in the aquarium, a wide variety of fish species are, and no one food will be sufficient to keep them all happy. Commercial foods are formulated to provide a good diet for the majority of commonly kept aquarium fish. These should form the basis of your fishes' diet, but you still need to feed other foods as well.

Live foods of various types can be purchased at most aquarium shops and should be fed to your fish once a week. Failing this you can use the frozen equivalents if live foods are unavailable at certain times of year. As an occasional substitute for live food, it does not really matter whether it is frozen blood-worms or black mosquito larvae. If it is going to be several months before live foods are available again (during harsh

ABOVE LEFT: Archer Fish (Toxotes opercularis) *use their caudal fin to generate sudden bursts of forward motion which enable them to jump clear of the water to catch low-flying insects.*

RIGHT: The Checker Barb (Barbus oligolepis) *is a typical omnivore, eating all kinds of food.*

winters this is often the case), then you must buy several types and feed them in rotation.

If you have fish that feed primarily on vegetable matter, you should buy a herbivore food and feed this from time to time instead of the normal flake food. Blanched lettuce leaves, boiled potato, and liquidized spinach are also good foods for these fish and should be fed every week.

Predators, on the other hand, should be fed with a carnivore food if they will eat it. If they are reluctant to eat commercial flake or granulated foods, try them on pieces of fish and if that fails, various live foods such as bloodworms, *Daphnia* or, for large fish,

earthworms. Some species, however, only eat live fish and must be fed these. Feeder fish are often found for sale in aquarium shops at a very cheap price. If you are thinking of having a predator like this, make sure you can afford to keep it and can secure a supply of food for it. (Some shops refuse to sell 20 Neon Tetras per week to a customer once they know they are food for another fish.)

REPRODUCTION IN FISH

From the very earliest days, it has not just been the lovely colors and graceful movement of aquarium fish that has captured aquarists' interest but the fascinating breeding habits of many

ABOVE: The female Lindu Duckbill (Xenopoecilus sarasorium) *has been carrying her eggs for 15 days. This method of brood care increases the embryo's chance of survival.*

species. Some people think all fish scatter their eggs over the gravel or in plants and that is the last the adults have to do with them. Aquarists, however, have found this is far from the truth for many species. While lots of fish do just scatter their eggs and swim away, others try to protect them from predators. The humble stickleback (*Gasterosteus aculeatus*), which children catch in their local park pond, builds a nest from plant material on the bottom and guards the eggs and young. Other species, such as the honey gourami (*Colisa chuna*), build a nest of bubbles at the water's surface and place their eggs in this. The male guards the nest until the young are able to fend for themselves.

Other species of fish go even further to protect their eggs by holding them in their mouth until they hatch. Quite a number of cichlids, gouramis, and some snakeheads use this method. Other species site their eggs on different parts of their body. Some species of catfish hold them on their lower lip, pipefish place them in a pouch on the male's stomach, while *Xenopoecilus sarasorium* have them hanging down from the female's vent on a thread like a bunch of grapes. All these methods increase the chance that the eggs will survive until they hatch.

One group of fish, however, make certain of this by holding the eggs inside their body until they are ready to

ABOVE: *The One-sided Livebearer* (Jenynsia lineata) *carries its young inside its body for up to eight weeks before giving birth to large, robust fry.*

hatch and then giving birth to free-swimming babies. These are the live-bearers which are very often the first species of fish an aquarist will breed. As a group they are very diverse. Most aquarists know them as four of the most popular aquarium fish: guppies, platies, mollies, and swordtails. These are only a small fraction of the fish that bear their young alive as a reproductive method. There are livebearers from every part of the world. In Russia livebearing fish live in deep-water lakes. The seas teem with livebearing fish, such as stingrays and many of the sharks.

FISH CONSERVATION

Freshwater fish are disappearing from the wild at an alarming rate, and unfortunately not very much is being done to stop their decline. In 1979 the American Fisheries Society produced a list of endangered and threatened fishes in the USA, Canada, and Mexico. This list was horrific enough with 251 species listed, but in 1989 a new list was produced which contained 364 species of fish needing protection because of their rarity. This is a staggering increase in just 10 years and gives you an idea of the scale of the problem.

The situation in the rest of the world is every bit as bad. Indeed there are now thousands of fish in trouble in the wild, and many of these have traditionally been popular aquarium fish. The 1994 I.U.C.N. (The World Conservation Union) Red List of threatened animals includes fish such as the cherry barb (*Barbus titteya*) and Celebes rainbow (*Telmatherina ladigesi*). Both are staples of the aquarium hobby being bred by the thousands on commercial fish farms. In the vast majority of cases (if not all), it is triple evils of habitat destruction, pollution, and exotic species introductions which have caused the decline in native fish populations.

Many scientists and conservationists have now come to the conclusion that captive breeding of fish is the only way many species are going to survive in the future, and it is clear that aquarists have a very important role to play in this. Even with all the zoos and public aquariums working together to maintain only those species already on the endangered lists, there are not enough resources to look after them all. Most people involved in endangered species protection work firmly expect the lists to more than double in the next 10 years. It is obvious that only by involving the millions of aquarists around the world are we going to save these fish from extinction.

How to use This Book

This book attempts to provide as much information as possible, on a wide variety of aquarium fish, in a clear and easily understood way. The species have been arranged into fish families or suborders with the species listed alphabetically (by scientific name) within each group.

Under species headings the information has been divided into a brief description, the distribution of the fish in the wild, and its temperament and care in captivity. Some details of how a particular fish breeds is also given and four "at a glance" symbols indicate the species suitability for a community aquarium, dietary requirements, area of the aquarium it occupies, and the temperature range needed for its well being.

Key to Symbols

Community

Yes   No

Dietary requirements

Carnivore   Omnivore   Herbivore

Area of aquarium

Surface   Midwater   Bottom

Temperature

79°f
▲
70°f

Carp-like fish
SUBORDER *Cyprinoidei*

This suborder of fish contains many of the very popular

aquarium fish, including barbs, danios, loaches, rasboras, and the

most popular aquarium fish in the world – goldfish. They have a

single dorsal fin usually situated midway down the body, and there are

no proper spines in the fins. They vary in size from fish which are

fully grown at just over 1 inch to those measuring about 5 feet.

Most members of this suborder are omnivores

and will eat all types of food. Some have barbels which they use to

grub around in the substrate searching for food, while others are

primarily midwater fish that take food in the water column

before it reaches the bottom.

SILVER SHARK *BALANTIOCHEILUS MELANOPTERUS*

DESCRIPTION The silver shark is covered with large silver scales that look like a polished mirror. The fins are silver to yellowish with bold black edges. It has a long streamlined body and can grow up to 1 ft.

DISTRIBUTION Southeast Asia.

TEMPERAMENT & CARE Despite being a large species, this fish is peaceful and will fit in well with other community fish. Due to its large size, it can only be kept in an aquarium which is at least 6½ ft. long and 1½ ft. wide.

79°f
▲
70°f

BREEDING Thought to be an egg-scatterer in common with other closely related fish.

CHECKER BARB *BARBUS OLIGOLEPIS*

DESCRIPTION A small barb species reaching a maximum size of just over 1½ in. As young fish they only have a faint, black, reticulated pattern to the body and a few black blotches along the flanks. Adult males have red fins edged in black.

DISTRIBUTION Indonesia and Sumatra.

TEMPERAMENT & CARE A peaceful, lively, shoaling species which is perfect for the community tank. Eats all foods and adapts well to most conditions.

BREEDING Egg-scatterer which spawns at first light. Males will choose a particular plant as the center of their territory and entice ripe females to spawn there. Once they have finished, the adults will devour all the eggs they can find.

79°f
▲
70°f

TINFOIL BARB *BARBUS SCHWANEFELDI*

81°f
▲
70°f

DESCRIPTION A deep-bodied, diamond-shaped fish which at 14 in. is one of the larger barb species. A beautiful glimmering silver fish, with black and red fins.

DISTRIBUTION Borneo, Malayan peninsula, Sumatra, and Thailand.

TEMPERAMENT & CARE Although a peaceful fish, it must be kept with fish of its own size in an aquarium at least 6½ ft. × 1½ ft. This is a schooling species which loves to swim against a current and needs strong filtration and large regular water changes to thrive. Will eat tender plants.

BREEDING Probably not bred by hobbyists because of its size. This species is an egg-scatterer producing several thousand eggs in a single spawning.

Schuberti Barb *Barbus semifasciolatus*

DESCRIPTION A strong-bodied barb with a golden body and reddish fins. Above the lateral line there are several black markings and a blotch in the caudal peduncle. The wild form has a green body with several vertical stripes, and an all-gold form has been bred. Maximum size is 3 in.

DISTRIBUTION The wild form is from southeast China.

TEMPERAMENT & CARE A robust, lively fish that holds its own in a community tank but is harmless to other fish. A hardy species which can live four or five years in captivity.

BREEDING Egg-scatterer, adults will spawn every two weeks and may produce several hundred eggs at each spawning.

Tiger Barb *Barbus tetrazona*

DESCRIPTION A deep-bodied barb which grows to a maximum size of nearly 3 in. The body is brownish yellow with four black vertical stripes running through the eye; just in front of, and behind, the dorsal fin; and through the caudal peduncle. Lots of different color morphs are known.

DISTRIBUTION Borneo, Indonesia, and Sumatra.

TEMPERAMENT & CARE A very lively species and possible bully. In a shoal they spend most of their time chasing each other but leave the other species alone. Very hardy, can live many years.

BREEDING Egg-scatterer laying about 200 eggs in plant thickets. Breeding takes place at first light and, once completed, the pair will eat any eggs they can find.

CHERRY BARB *BARBUS TITTEYA*

DESCRIPTION A beautiful small barb (2 in.), lovely cherry red males and pinkish brown females. A dark lateral line runs through the eye to the caudal peduncle. This is strongly marked in females and immature males but fades in adult males.

DISTRIBUTION Sri Lanka.

TEMPERAMENT & CARE A very peaceful barb and good community fish. This is less of a schooling fish than many barbs and is best kept in pairs. A hardy robust species that will live many years in captivity.

BREEDING Egg-scatterer, lays eggs in plant thickets. Up to 300 eggs are produced in one spawning. The parents are avid egg eaters and will devour all they can.

CLOWN LOACH *BOTIA MACRACANTHUS*

DESCRIPTION A flat-bellied, high-backed loach with four pairs of barbels. Yellow-bodied with three black bands running vertically through it. The first passes through the eye, the second is just in front of the dorsal fin, and the third starts in the dorsal fin, passes through the body, and ends in the anal fin. The other fins are reddish orange. It develops to a maximum size of 1 ft.

DISTRIBUTION Borneo, Indonesia, and Sumatra.

TEMPERAMENT & CARE A peaceful species cohabiting well with fish of a similar size. Feels more secure if kept with group and provided with some hiding places.

BREEDING A seasonal egg-scatterer. Breeds during the rainy season in fast-flowing waters. Rarely bred in captivity.

CHAIN BOTIA *BOTIA SIDTHIMUNKI*

DESCRIPTION A slender golden yellow fish with a black horizontal stripe from the eye to caudal peduncle and another across the back. About eight vertical bars are also found along the flanks. Maximum size just over 2 in.
DISTRIBUTION Northern India and Thailand.
TEMPERAMENT & CARE A peaceful schooling fish, ideal for community tanks. It is hardy, eats all foods, and even hunts out the scraps that fall between the pieces of gravel.

79°f
▲
72°f

BREEDING Only recently bred in captivity for the first time. It is said to be an egg-scatterer which lays its eggs into the gravel and only spawns at certain times of the year.

ZEBRA DANIO *BRACHYDANIO RERIO*

DESCRIPTION A long slender species with lovely blue horizontal stripes the full length of its body and into the fins. Males have gold between the blue and females have silver coloration. Maximum size 2 in.
DISTRIBUTION Eastern India.
TEMPERAMENT & CARE A peaceful, fast-moving, shoaling fish which is best kept in groups of six or more. They eat all foods and are very hardy. Long-finned and various color forms are known, including the leopard danio (*Brachydanio frankei*) which was thought to be a separate species for many years.

BREEDING Easy egg-scatterer which will produce up to 100 eggs per spawning.

77°f
▲
70°f

GOLDFISH *CARASSIUS AURATUS*

DESCRIPTION The wild form is a bronzy brown color with typical carp-shaped body and single tail. From this wild fish, golden mutations were selectively bred and later different fin forms. Today there are over 100 different varieties. Males develop white pimples on the leading edges of the pectoral fins and gill covers during the breeding season.

DISTRIBUTION The wild form probably originated in China but it has now been introduced to habitats the world over.

79°f
▲
48°f

TEMPERAMENT & CARE Peaceful coldwater species. Needs a large aquarium with good filtration and aeration.

BREEDING Lays its eggs in plants during the summer months. Large pairs may produce up to 1,000 eggs per spawning.

GIANT DANIO *DANIO AEQUIPINNATUS*

DESCRIPTION A torpedo-shaped species with a mottled blue and yellow body. The fins are generally clear to grayish with a dark blotch in the middle of the caudal fin. Maximum size 4 in.

DISTRIBUTION West coast of India and Sri Lanka.

TEMPERAMENT & CARE A very lively, gregarious species which likes to be part of a shoal. They prefer clean, well-oxygenated water filtered by a power filter producing water movement. They eat all foods but feed mainly from the surface.

BREEDING Easy egg-scatterer which spawns in plant thickets and produces up to 300 eggs.

81°f
▲
70°f

RED-TAILED BLACK SHARK *EPALZEORHYNCHUS BICOLOR*

81°f
▲
73°f

DESCRIPTION A very striking fish with a black body and bright red tail. The body is torpedo-shaped, and the dorsal fin stands up high like a shark's. Maximum size 6 in.

DISTRIBUTION Thailand.

TEMPERAMENT & CARE An aggressive territorial species which is often sold as a community fish but can cause mayhem by attacking anything that comes into its territory.

It likes a cave or other hiding place and will eat all foods that sink to the bottom.

BREEDING Rarely bred but said to lay its eggs in a rocky hollow.

FLYING FOX *EPALZEORHYNCHUS KALLOPTERUS*

DESCRIPTION A very long slender species with a lovely black stripe running through the eye into the caudal fin. The body is brown above the stripe and white below. The dorsal and anal fins have black blotches in them. Maximum size 6 in.

DISTRIBUTION Borneo, Indonesia, Northern India, and Sumatra.

TEMPERAMENT & CARE While basically a peaceful fish, it is territorial against other flying foxes, so should be kept singly and with access to a cave or other hideaway.

BREEDING Unknown.

81°f
▲
70°f

SUCKING LOACH *GYRINOCHEILUS AYMONIERI*

DESCRIPTION A very strange-looking creature with a flat underside and modified mouth parts. The mouth is a sucking disk with which the fish holds on to rocks, the aquarium sides, or other surfaces. A brown stripe runs through the eye to the caudal fin, above this the body is golden brown and below it silver. Maximum size nearly 10 in.

DISTRIBUTION Northern India and Thailand.

TEMPERAMENT & CARE A territorial species as an adult. Can become a problem in a community aquarium by attacking any fish that enters its territory. It is usually included as an algae eater but there are many other species which will do this job and are not aggressive.

BREEDING Unknown.

81°f
▲
70°f

ORFE *LEUCISCUS IDUS*

DESCRIPTION A long slender-bodied fish with a dull brownish body and silvery white ventral region. A beautiful golden variety (golden orfe) with reddish fins is very popular. Maximum size said to be over 3 ft. but most only reach 1½ ft. in captivity.

DISTRIBUTION Found throughout most of continental Europe.

TEMPERAMENT & CARE A peaceful coldwater species ideal for large ponds and sometimes kept in aquariums. They eat all foods but, when adults, prefer live insects and small fish.

70°f
▲
39°f

BREEDING Spawns in late spring and early summer among plants in shallow water.

CHINESE WEATHER LOACH *MISGURNUS ANGUILLICAUDATUS*

DESCRIPTION Long and slender with a down-turned mouth having barbels around it. The coloration tends to be individual with many different races in the wild. Body color is often light brown becoming white along the belly, overlaid with brown spots and mottling over the whole body. Maximum size nearly 10 in.

DISTRIBUTION China, Korea, Japan, and parts of Siberia.

TEMPERAMENT & CARE A peaceful, nocturnal bottom-dweller, stays half buried in the substrate during the day. Hides in caves or rocks. Feeds from the bottom. Must be specially fed in a community tank after the lights have been turned off or it may waste away.

BREEDING Lays eggs in plant thickets from April to July.

77°f
▲
39°f

RED SHINER *NOTROPIS LUTRENSIS*

DESCRIPTION A truly beautiful coldwater fish. Males are a lovely sky-blue color with red fins. When in breeding condition, these colors are heightened and white pimples appear over the head and pectoral fins. Maximum size 3 in.

DISTRIBUTION California, Colorado, Illinois, Iowa, Minnesota, and Wyoming, as well as parts of northern Mexico.

TEMPERAMENT & CARE A shoaling coldwater species which must have clean, cool, well-oxygenated water. Can be kept in an outdoor pond during a winter that is not harsh, but displays well in an aquarium where the lovely colors can be appreciated.

77°f
59°f

BREEDING Egg-scatterer that is rarely bred in captivity. Spawns during the summer months only.

COOLIE LOACH *PANGIO KUHLII SUMATRANUS*

DESCRIPTION A very long slender snake-like species with a down-turned mouth and several pairs of barbels. The body color is pinkish gray with chocolate-brown bars across the back and down the flanks. Several different subspecies are known with different color patterns. Maximum size 4 in.

DISTRIBUTION Borneo, Java, Malaysia, Sumatra, Singapore, and Thailand.

TEMPERAMENT & CARE A secretive, nocturnal species foraging for food when the lights are out. Needs plenty of hiding places and will even bury itself in the gravel or under subgravel filter plates. Make sure they are fed at night.

BREEDING A seasonal breeder which lays green eggs at night among the roots and stems of floating plants.

81°f
72°f

HARLEQUIN   *RASBORA HETEROMORPHA*

81°f
▲
70°f

DESCRIPTION A deep-bodied, almost diamond-shaped rasbora with a pinkish body color and large triangular black blotch in the rear half of the body. There are several similar species (*espei* and *hengeli*) but this one has the deepest body and largest black blotch. Maximum size almost 2 in.

DISTRIBUTION Malaysia, Singapore, Sumatra, and Thailand.

TEMPERAMENT & CARE A perfect community fish which, although quite small, can cope with larger more boisterous species. Eats all foods and lives for several years in captivity.

BREEDING Lays eggs on the underside of broad-leafed plants or in plant thickets. During spawning, the pair embrace while upside down.

SCISSORTAIL *RASBORA TRILINEATA*

DESCRIPTION A torpedo-shaped species with silvery body. Along the side from below the dorsal fin there is a black line which finishes in the caudal peduncle, and in each lobe of the caudal fin are black and yellow blotches. Maximum size 4 in.

DISTRIBUTION Borneo, Malaysia, and Sumatra.

TEMPERAMENT & CARE A very peaceful community fish which is lively and likes to be part of a shoal. Despite growing quite large, it can be kept with small fish and will live many years in captivity.

81°f
70°f

BREEDING Spawns in plant thickets where its adhesive eggs remain attached to the plants until they hatch.

EXCLAMATION SPOT RASBORA *RASBORA UROPHTHALMA*

DESCRIPTION One of the miniatures of the fish world, adults grow to under 1 in. Both sexes have a dark band running down the side from behind the gill cover to in front of the caudal peduncle. Here a black spot edged in gold shines out. The male's fins have red and black markings. There is a reddish hue to the body.

DISTRIBUTION Sumatra.

TEMPERAMENT & CARE Despite its small size, it copes well in a community of small fish. Its small mouth can only take small foods such as crushed flake and newly hatched brine shrimp or sieved *Daphnia*.

BREEDING Lays eggs among dense plant growth in very soft acidic water.

81°f
70°f

BITTERLING *RHODEUS SERICEUS AMERUS*

DESCRIPTION A deep-bodied species. Females have a silvery body with a bluish sheen. Males have red in the dorsal and anal fins plus a red iris to the top of the eye. Maximum size 3 in.

DISTRIBUTION Much of Europe and into western Asia.

TEMPERAMENT & CARE A fascinating, lively, coldwater fish eating all foods and fitting in well with other fish of a similar size.

BREEDING One of the most unusual members of this group. Females develop a huge ovipositor during the breeding season which deposits eggs inside a swan mussel. Here eggs and young develop until they are about four weeks old.

75°f
61°f

WHITE CLOUD MOUNTAIN MINNOW *TANICHTHYS ALBONUBES*

DESCRIPTION The slender body is reddish brown paling to white on the belly. From the eye to the caudal peduncle, there is a lovely iridescent green stripe which glows when the fish are young. The fins have splashes of red and may be edged in green. Maximum size just over 1½ in.

DISTRIBUTION Southern China, particularly in the streams near the White Mountain.

TEMPERAMENT & CARE A lively schooling fish. It does well in a tropical aquarium, a coldwater tank indoors, or an outside pond during the summer months. Eats all foods and likes clean, well-oxygenated water.

BREEDING Egg-scatterer that spawns in plant thickets.

75°f
63°f

Catfish
*Suborder **Siluroidei***

Catfish can be found almost all over the world

and inhabit just about every part of the aquatic habitat. Some species

are predominantly plant-eaters, while others are predators that

will eat anything living. Only a few species live in marine habitats,

and these are said to move into brackish water to breed.

Many species care for their eggs and young,

and there are great differences between the reproductive

strategies employed.

There are thought to be over 1,000 species in the suborder,

all of which are scaleless and have a Weberian ossicle.

The Weberian ossicle is also known as the Weberian apparatus.

This was derived from the first four vertebrae which link the

inner ear to the swim bladder and help amplify sound.

BRISTLE-NOSE CATFISH *ANCISTRUS DOLICHOPTERUS*

DESCRIPTION A strange looking, sucker-mouthed catfish with large branching bristles around the mouth and on the male's head. The body color is mottled brown as are the fins. The front rays of the pectoral fins are thick, sharp spines. Maximum size nearly 5 in.

DISTRIBUTION Fast-flowing streams of the Amazon.

TEMPERAMENT & CARE A nocturnal fish rarely seen during the day and only then when it is hungry or if the water quality has deteriorated. Feed lots of vegetable matter like lettuce leaves.

BREEDING The pair spawn under rocks or bog wood after which the female is chased away and the male sits on the eggs and young until they are large enough to take care of themselves.

81°f
70°f

BRONZE CORYDORAS *CORYDORAS AENEUS*

DESCRIPTION The most popular corydoras species. Large iridescent green patch on each side of body from the gill cover to the caudal peduncle. The mouth is down-turned and has several pairs of barbels. Maximum size 2½ in.

DISTRIBUTION Brazil, Colombia, Ecuador, Peru, Trinidad, and Venezuela.

TEMPERAMENT & CARE An active species, even during the day, this is a good catfish species for a community aquarium. It will never hassle other fish and rarely succumbs to disease. Tablet, frozen, and live foods should be included in their diet.

BREEDING Plasters eggs over the aquarium back and sides as well as on broad-leafed plants.

81°f
70°f

BANDED CORYDORAS *CORYDORAS BARBATUS*

81°f
70°f

DESCRIPTION A long-snouted corydoras with a golden body mottled with brown. When fully mature, males have extended dorsal and pectoral fin spines. Maximum size 4 in.

DISTRIBUTION Brazil near Rio de Janeiro and São Paulo.

TEMPERAMENT & CARE A peaceful fish which does well in an aquarium with gentle species and soft acidic water conditions. They eat any food which settles on the bottom, but most need some live food in the diet to be kept in perfect health.

BREEDING Spawns in groups of two or more pairs and produces up to 100 eggs per spawning. These are laid in clumps on the aquarium sides like small bunches of grapes.

PEPPERED CORYDORAS *CORYDORAS PALEATUS*

DESCRIPTION A brown mottled species of corydoras that is one of the most popular aquarium fish. Females are decidedly plumper and males have longer and more pointed dorsal and pectoral fins. In wild strains, males have very long extensions to these fins. Maximum size nearly 3 in.

DISTRIBUTION Argentina, Brazil, and Uruguay.

TEMPERAMENT & CARE A peaceful, hardy fish which fits in well in any community tank. Eats all foods but particularly likes small worms, such as white worms.

81°f
▲
70°f

BREEDING Plasters eggs over the aquarium sides and on broad-leafed plants. Will also spawn in a clump of Java moss or a spawning mop.

WHIPTAIL CATFISH *FARLOWELLA ACUS*

DESCRIPTION A very long, slender sucker-mouth catfish, twig-like in appearance. A very long snout sticks way out in front of the mouth. The body color is light brown with a dark brown stripe running along the sides. Maximum size nearly 5 in.

DISTRIBUTION Amazon.

TEMPERAMENT & CARE A shy, retiring species which should be kept with small quiet fish in a tank that has an abundant growth of algae. Most specimens will starve to death in captivity without such an adequate supply.

BREEDING Pairs spawn on vertical surfaces. The male guards the eggs from harm. When they are ready to hatch, he helps break them out of the egg shells.

82°f
▲
73°f

SPOTTED HOPLO *HOPLOSTERNUM THORACATUM*

DESCRIPTION A mahogany brown fish with dark, almost black, blotches over the body and fins. The body shape is long, and the mouth is forward-pointing with three pairs of long whiskers. Maximum size 6 in.

DISTRIBUTION Brazil, Guyana, Martinique, Paraguay, Peru, and Trinidad.

TEMPERAMENT & CARE Most active in the evening but may take food during the day. Usually peaceful and harmless to tankmates, but during the breeding season, males become territorial and will be aggressive toward other fish.

81°f
73°f

BREEDING Builds a bubble nest under floating vegetation into which the pair lay several hundred eggs. The male then protects the eggs until the fry hatch out and swim off.

PLECOSTOMUS *HYPOSTOMUS PUNCTATUS*

DESCRIPTION This is a large (1 ft.), flat-bodied, sucker-mouth catfish which has a very large sail-like dorsal fin. The first rays of the pectoral fins are thick spines that can puncture a polyethylene bag with ease and will become entangled in a net. The body color is an overall mottled brown, and the fins have a net-like pattern over them.

DISTRIBUTION Brazil.

TEMPERAMENT & CARE A peaceful community fish which is rarely active during the day and prefers to hide away in caves. A vegetarian that eats all kinds of vegetable matter, including aquarium plants.

BREEDING Spawns in a tunnel dug into the river bank. The male guards the eggs.

81°f
70°f

GHOST CATFISH *KRYPTOPTERUS BICIRRHIS*

DESCRIPTION A peculiar-looking transparent fish with long slender body and a forward-pointing pair of barbels. The body sac is silvery, and all the bone structure can be seen through the sides of the fish. Maximum size 5 in.

DISTRIBUTION Borneo, India, Indonesia, Malaysia, Sumatra, and Thailand.

TEMPERAMENT & CARE Peaceful shoaling fish which likes a strong water current. Can be sensitive to poor water quality and needs a varied diet, including some live foods.

82°f
▲
73°f

BREEDING Egg-scatterer which lays its eggs in plant thickets. Rarely bred in the aquarium.

BLUE-EYED PLECOSTOMUS *PANAQUE SUTTONI*

DESCRIPTION The black body and fins contrast strongly with the brilliant blue eye of this sucker-mouth catfish. The caudal fin is sickle-shaped, and the dorsal is large and held almost vertically. Maximum size 7 in.

DISTRIBUTION Colombia and Guyana.

TEMPERAMENT & CARE A quiet, shy fish which needs plenty of caves to hide in, and clean, well-filtered water. Must have aeration to raise the oxygen content and be fed with plenty of vegetable matter. Loves cucumber and peas.

BREEDING Unknown.

81°f
▲
73°f

POLKA-DOT CATFISH *SYNODONTIS ANGELICUS*

81°f
▲
73°f

DESCRIPTION The velvety black body contrasts sharply with the white polka dots which cover the body. The fins are banded black and white and the first ray of the pectoral fin is a sharp spine. Maximum size 7 in.
DISTRIBUTION Cameroon and Zaire.

TEMPERAMENT & CARE Peaceful schooling, nocturnal species which likes to hide in caves during the day. At night it digs in the substrate searching for food and will uproot plants. Needs some live foods in its diet to thrive.
BREEDING Unknown but possibly seasonal pit-spawner.

Characins

SUBORDER *Characoidei*

There are a huge number of characin species in the world,

many of which are yet to be described by science. At the moment,

there are about 1,000 species known from South America and at least

200 from the African continent, but more are being discovered all the

time. The fact that they are found on both continents helps prove

that Africa and South America were joined at one stage and that

the characoidei had already evolved at this time. Since the continental

split is thought to have occurred in Mesozoic times when Dinosaurs

still lived, this means characins were swimming around in the rivers

with these fantastic reptiles.

MARBLED HEADSTANDER *ABRAMITES HYPSELONOTUS*

DESCRIPTION A deep-bodied fish with a marbled brown and fawn body. This species has a habit of swimming with its head down and resting almost vertically with the tail uppermost. Maximum size nearly 5 in.

DISTRIBUTION Found throughout the Amazon and Orinoco river systems.

TEMPERAMENT & CARE A loner which can be kept in a mixed community tank of similar-sized fish but not with its own species. Likes plenty of cover in the form of bog wood and plants but will eat new shoots.

BREEDING Unknown in captivity.

81°f
▲
73°f

STRIPED ANOSTOMUS *ANOSTOMUS ANOSTOMUS*

DESCRIPTION A slender-bodied fish with yellow and black stripes running the full body length. There is a splash of blood red at the base of the dorsal and caudal fins. Maximum size 6 in.

DISTRIBUTION Colombia, Guyana, and Venezuela.

TEMPERAMENT & CARE Best kept in a large school of six or more fish or as individual specimens in a community aquarium. Will eat all foods but will nibble plants when nothing else is available.

BREEDING Lays adhesive eggs in plant thickets near the surface.

81°f
▲
73°f

BLOODFIN *APHOCHARAX ANISITSI*

DESCRIPTION A lovely silvery fish with blood red in the pelvic, anal, and caudal fins. It used to be very common in the hobby but is rarely imported today. It can live up to 10 years in captivity and grows to 2 in. in body length.

DISTRIBUTION Argentina.

TEMPERAMENT & CARE Peaceful schooling fish which is constantly on the move. Eats anything and is very hardy. Likes plenty of swimming room, but some plant thickets should also be included in the aquarium setup.

81°f
▲
72°f

BREEDING Easy egg-scatterer that lays its eggs in plant thickets near the surface.

BLIND CAVE TETRA *ASTYANAX FASCIATUS MEXICANUS*

DESCRIPTION This is the cave form of *Astynax fasciatus mexicanus*. As with most cave fish, the eyes are reduced to almost nothing and all pigmentation has been lost. The result is a pinkish fish with clear fins and no visible eyes. Maximum size 3 in.

DISTRIBUTION Found in underground rivers flowing through Mexican cave systems.

TEMPERAMENT & CARE Peaceful fish which, despite having no eyes, can find food as quickly as other fish. Can be kept in most community tanks and will eat all foods.

BREEDING Scatters eggs in open water. Spawning usually follows a water change.

79°f
▲
68°f

MARBLED HATCHETFISH *CARNEGIELLA STRIGATA STRIGATA*

DESCRIPTION The body is very deep and resembles the head of an ax. They have very large pectoral fins that look a lot like wings and perform the same function, enabling this fish to skim across the water surface when frightened. The body color is marbled black, silver, and brown, and the fish grows to only just over 1½ in.

DISTRIBUTION Peru.

TEMPERAMENT & CARE Peaceful, although skittish fish which should be kept in a shoal of six or more. Will eat all floating foods and loves wingless fruit flies and other insects that float on the surface.

BREEDING Scatters semiadhesive eggs among floating plant roots.

BLACK WIDOW TETRA *GYMNOCORYMBUS TERNETZI*

DESCRIPTION A deep-bodied tetra with black dorsal and anal fins and a silvery body with several vertical black markings. The anal fin is very large and has many rays in it. Maximum size 2 in.

DISTRIBUTION Bolivia.

TEMPERAMENT & CARE Peaceful shoaling fish which is ideal for the community tank. Likes some plant cover and tends to hide among this as it gets older. Eats all foods but likes some live food in the diet.

BREEDING Prolific fish which scatters its eggs in plant thickets.

BLACK NEON TETRA *HYPHESSOBRYCON HERBERTAXELRODI*

DESCRIPTION Typical tetra with a glowing green line from behind the eye to the caudal peduncle. Below this the body is black, becoming silvery on the belly. The upper iris is red, and the fish grows to a maximum size of only just over 1½ in.

DISTRIBUTION Mato Grosso, Brazil.

TEMPERAMENT & CARE Peaceful community fish which will form schools with other fish. Likes insects and other meaty foods in its diet and will eat newborn livebearers.

BREEDING Needs very soft and acidic water to breed in. Thrives on lots of live foods. Spawns in plant thickets.

EMPEROR TETRA *NEMATOBRYCON PALMERI*

DESCRIPTION A beautiful fish with iridescent blue sheen to the body and trident-shaped tail. Below the lateral line, the body is black, becoming white on the belly. The iris of the eye is blue in males and green in females. Maximum size just over 2 in.

DISTRIBUTION Colombia.

TEMPERAMENT & CARE Peaceful fish which tends to swim around plant thickets in groups of three or four. Males will occasionally spar, but no real damage is done during these encounters.

BREEDING Spawns in plants near the surface, but the semiadhesive eggs often fall into the substrate and continue their development there.

NEON TETRA *PARACHEIRODON INNESI*

82°f
72°f

DESCRIPTION A neon blue line runs from the eye to just before the origin of the adipose fin. The lower half of the body is silver in front and blood red toward the rear. This is one of the best known aquarium fish, and it grows to only just over 1½ in.

DISTRIBUTION Peru.

TEMPERAMENT & CARE Peaceful community fish which, despite its small size, can hold its own with larger fish. Likes to have some planted areas to retire to. Hardy and will live several years in captivity.

BREEDING Spawns in open water after which the eggs sink into the substrate and hatch the next day. Must have very soft acidic water for the eggs to hatch.

CONGO TETRA *PHENACOGRAMMUS INTERRUPTUS*

DESCRIPTION A beautiful characin with a rainbow of colors on the body. Males develop extensions to the dorsal, anal, and the center of the caudal fin. Full grown males reach nearly 3 in. and females nearly 2½ in.
DISTRIBUTION Zaire.
TEMPERAMENT & CARE Peaceful although somewhat timid schooling fish which likes lots of open swimming space combined with some areas of dense plant growth. Eats all foods from the top and midwater area of the tank and will nibble plant shoots.

BREEDING Scatters nonadhesive eggs in shallow open water. Most spawnings occur at first light.

RED-BELLIED PIRANHA *SERRASALMUS NATTERERI*

DESCRIPTION A deep-bodied fish with a black-spotted silver body when young. At this age there is a red patch behind the gill cover, and the anal fin is red. As an adult the body is an overall brownish silver and the throat and ventral region are blood red. Maximum size 11 in.
DISTRIBUTION Widely distributed throughout the Amazon and Orinoco rivers.
TEMPERAMENT & CARE A nasty, vicious predator which will bite anything which threatens it. While it likes to feed on live fish, most specimens will learn to take dead foods, like pieces of fish or meat.

BREEDING Pit-spawner in which the pair initially guard the nest but eventually the male chases his mate away.

Once the fry are free-swimming, he should be removed.

Cichlids

Suborder Percoidei, Family Cichlidae

Cichlids are a very large family of freshwater fish

distributed throughout Africa, Central and South America, India,

and parts of the Middle East. Various estimates exist of the

number of species contained in the family, and there are in excess of

900 described species throughout the world. Most protect their

eggs in some way, and many make interesting aquarium fish.

Few species are good community fish.

In recent times, several species of tilapia have been

introduced all over the world as useful food fish. These, unfortunately,

have caused the rapid decline of native species.

PANDA DWARF CICHLID *APISTOGRAMMA NIJSSENI*

DESCRIPTION Males are bluish with a yellow belly and orange-edged caudal fin. Females are yellow with greenish black blotches and look like a completely different species. Maximum size for males is nearly 2½ in. and for females just over 1½ in.

DISTRIBUTION Peru.

TEMPERAMENT & CARE A somewhat timid territorial species that can only be combined with quiet, peaceful fish. Likes lots of plants in the tank and areas where each male may define his own territory. Include some caves made out of rocks.

81°f
73°f

BREEDING Cave-spawner. The female looks after the eggs, the male guards the territory.

OSCAR *ASTRONOTUS OCELLATUS*

DESCRIPTION This large (1 ft.) cichlid has matt scales. They are mottled dark and light brown to gray with splashes of orange, particularly in the fins. A "peacock's eye" adorns the caudal peduncle and is edged in bright orange. Several color forms exist.

DISTRIBUTION Amazon Basin.

TEMPERAMENT & CARE While not really aggressive, this fish forms a nuclear family which guards its own territory and can only be housed in a large aquarium. This must have a deep substrate and some rockwork.

BREEDING Open-spawners which lay their eggs on a rock. The adult pair look after their young until they are able to take care of themselves. Spawns of 2,000 are known.

72°f
82°f

STRIPED PIKE CICHLID *CRENICICHLA STRIGATA*

DESCRIPTION A large (16 in.) slender-bodied fish with horizontal stripes running the full length of the body when young. These stripes fade as they mature, and females develop a red stomach.

DISTRIBUTION Brazil & Guyana.

TEMPERAMENT & CARE A large predator which can only be kept by itself or with others of its own species if they are reared together. Needs a very large aquarium with lots of roots and rockwork to provide hiding places.

BREEDING Cave-spawner in which both parents care for the eggs and young.

82°f
▲
73°f

JEWEL CICHLID *HEMICHROMIS BIMACULATUS*

DESCRIPTION A chunky-bodied, medium-sized cichlid reaching a maximum size of 6 in. As a juvenile, the body is a dull olive green with three black spots on the sides. In breeding condition, they turn a beautiful blood red with blue spots.

DISTRIBUTION Coastal Africa from Guinea to Liberia.

TEMPERAMENT & CARE Aggressive territorial species that can only be kept as a breeding pair or group of youngsters. Likes a deep substrate to dig in and plenty of caves and rocks. Plants are often dug up.

BREEDING Eggs are laid in caves, and both parents nurture them. Later the fry are moved to pits dug in the substrate.

82°f
▲
73°f

REGAN'S JULIE *JULIDOCHROMIS REGANI*

DESCRIPTION A slender-bodied cichlid which grows to a maximum size of nearly 4 in, although males are usually smaller. They have a lovely yellow and black horizontally striped body.

DISTRIBUTION Lake Tanganyika.

TEMPERAMENT & CARE A territorial species which is best kept as a breeding pair and their offspring. Include lots of caves and rockwork and some hardy well-rooted plants for cover.

81°f
75°f

BREEDING Spawns in caves. The pair move free-swimming fry into a pit dug in the substrate.

LYRETAIL CICHLID *NEOLAMPROLOGUS BRICHARDI*

DESCRIPTION A very pretty cichlid with a distinctive lyre-shaped tail. The body is gray with a dark line through the eye and a black spot on the operculum. Just in front of this spot is a golden blotch. Maximum size 4 in.

DISTRIBUTION Tanganyika.

TEMPERAMENT & CARE Likes to form schools of its own species and will tolerate other similar-sized peaceful fish. Must have very hard alkaline water and needs to be fed plenty of live foods.

BREEDING Spawns in caves after which the female guards the eggs. Later broods are cared for by their older siblings as well as their parents.

81°f
72°f

AURATUS MBUNA *MELANOCHROMIS AURATUS*

DESCRIPTION A beautiful slender-bodied cichlid with very differently colored sexes. Females are golden yellow with two black horizontal stripes and several white ones. Mature males are black with two white horizontal stripes. Maximum size 4 in.

DISTRIBUTION Lake Malawi.

TEMPERAMENT & CARE An aggressive territorial species which must be kept in a Malawi cichlid tank with lots of rockwork and hiding places. Can be kept as a breeding group on their own, in which case combine one male with at least four females.

79°f
▲
72°f

BREEDING Males mate with any ripe female who then picks up the eggs and broods them in her mouth. She also cares for the fry for a week after they initially leave her mouth.

RAM *PAPILIOCHROMIS RAMIREZI*

DESCRIPTION A beautiful small (nearly 2½ in.) cichlid with an overall blue body color and yellow to red stomach. A large black spot adorns the middle of the body, and a vertical black stripe runs through the eye. The fins are reddish with electric blue spangles, and the front rays of the dorsal are black.

DISTRIBUTION Colombia and Venezuela.

TEMPERAMENT & CARE A peaceful community fish which loves lots of plant growth and places to hide, but will spend most of the time out and about once it has settled in. Usually lives only three years.

BREEDING Open-spawner with both parents protecting the eggs and young. Once the babies are free-swimming, the parents move them into a breeding pit.

82°f
▲
73°f

KRIBENSIS *PELVICACHROMIS PULCHER*

81°f
▲
70°f

DESCRIPTION One of the most underrated small (3 in.) cichlids available. As young fish they are a dull olive color with a dark stripe running from the eye to the caudal peduncle. Once mature, however, they develop a beautiful red stomach and females have lime green patches before and after the red area.
DISTRIBUTION Nigeria.

TEMPERAMENT & CARE A peaceful territorial species which will live happily in a community tank that contains rocky hiding places. Likes a well-planted tank and will dig in the substrate but rarely uproot plants.
BREEDING Cave-spawners, the female looks after eggs and young while the male guards the territory.

ZEBRA MBUNA *PSEUDOTROPHEUS ZEBRA*

DESCRIPTION A typical Mbuna species which has a huge range of different color forms. The typical color is blue with lots of vertical black bars on the body and a few false egg spots on the anal fin. Some color forms are gold with black blotches, and others have no black markings. Maximum size nearly 5 in.

DISTRIBUTION Lake Malawi.

TEMPERAMENT & CARE An aggressive species suitable for its own species tank or a mixed Malawi tank. Needs lots of rocks and hiding places. Keep one male to three females.

79°f
▲
72°f

BREEDING Male mates with any ripe female. The eggs are mouthbrooded by the female who tends the fry for a week after she has released them.

ANGELFISH *PTEROPHYLLUM SCALARE*

DESCRIPTION A deep-bodied fish with extended dorsal, anal, and pelvic fins. The caudal fin also has filaments from its top and bottom lobe. Many different color patterns have been developed, but the wild form is silver with four vertical stripes. Maximum size 4 in.

DISTRIBUTION Amazon basin.

TEMPERAMENT & CARE As young fish they form a school and spend much of their time together. Once mature they form pairs which have their own territory. Basically peaceful but will eat any very small fish and, when large, may bully tankmates.

BREEDING Open-spawners which lay their eggs on a plant leaf or other suitable vertical surface. The pair look after their eggs and the young.

81°f
▲
72°f

GREEN DISCUS *SYMPHYSODON AEQUIFASCIATUS*

DESCRIPTION A discus-shaped fish bred in a variety of color forms. The wild form has a brownish body with faint vertical bars. The iris is red. Throughout the fins and over much of the head, there is a green pattern. Maximum size 6 in.

DISTRIBUTION Amazon.

TEMPERAMENT & CARE Considered difficult and should be kept in a tank on its own. Needs a deep, well-planted aquarium and soft acidic water. The diet should contain lots of live food.

BREEDING Open-spawner which lays its eggs on any suitable vertical surface. The pair look after the eggs and fry, which feed on secretions from the parents' bodies.

Gobies and related fish

SUBORDER Gobioidei

This is a very large group of fish which have two

dorsal fins and are commonly found in brackish and marine habitats.

Some species have adapted to freshwater and are kept by aquarists.

Most have their pelvic fins fused into a single fin that is used as a

sucking disk, and many have a reduced swim bladder so that they

scuttle about the bottom. One of the biggest problems with this group

is that they rarely take commercial foods and need to be fed live or

frozen foods if they are to survive in captivity.

BUMBLEBEE GOBY *BRACHYGOBIUS XANTHOZONA*

DESCRIPTION A pretty little (just over 1½ in.) fish with a yellow body with four vertical black bars. It has a reduced swim bladder so spends most of its time on the bottom, but the pelvic fins form a sucking disk with which it can hang on to the tank sides if it wishes.
DISTRIBUTION Thailand and Vietnam.
TEMPERAMENT & CARE A gentle, timid species that can only be combined with other small peaceful fish. A territorial species which chases other species off. Add 1 tablespoon of sea salt to each 2 gallons of water and feed only live foods.
BREEDING Cave-spawner with the male guarding the eggs and fry.

81°f
▲
72°f

PEACOCK GOBY *TATEURNDINA OCELLICAUDA*

DESCRIPTION Beautiful blue goby with red and yellow markings in the body and fins. In the caudal peduncle is a black spot, and the ventral region of the body is yellow. This fish has a normal swim bladder. Maximum size 2 in.
DISTRIBUTION New Guinea.
TEMPERAMENT & CARE Peaceful hardy fish which fits in well in a small fish community. Likes plenty of plant growth, rocks, or other objects to hide in and around. Rarely accepts commercial foods and should therefore be fed live foods to be at their best.

BREEDING Cave-spawner with the male looking after the eggs.

81°f
▲
72°f

Gouramis and other labyrinth fish
Suborder *Anabantoidei*

Gouramis and other labyrinth fish have developed

an organ called the labyrinth that enables them to take gulps of

atmospheric air and extract oxygen from it. This means they can

survive in very badly polluted water when other fish would die.

Two main methods of reproduction are used in the group:

mouthbrooding and bubble nesting. In the latter, the males build

a nest of bubbles coated in saliva into which the eggs are placed.

In mouthbrooders, the eggs are taken into the male's mouth and held

until the fry are free-swimming.

SIAMESE FIGHTING FISH *BETTA SPLENDENS*

82°f
▲
70°f

DESCRIPTION An incredibly beautiful fish. The males have extended fins of red, blue, black, white, green, or any combination of these colors. In females the colors tend to be muted, and the fins are short. A twin-tailed form is known. Maximum size nearly 2½ in.

DISTRIBUTION Cambodia and Thailand.

TEMPERAMENT & CARE While the males will attack and kill each other, several females can usually be housed in one tank. In a normal community tank with fast-moving fish, the males are often subjected to bullying. Use plant cover to reduce this problem.

BREEDING Builds a bubble nest. If the female is not ready to spawn, she will be damaged or killed.

DWARF GOURAMI *COLISA LALIA*

DESCRIPTION A deep-bodied, small (2 in.) fish which is truly beautiful. Females are silvery with blue vertical bands and males are rusty red with the same blue bands. The male throat is also blue, and the fins are mottled red and blue. There are several color forms.

DISTRIBUTION India and possibly Borneo.

TEMPERAMENT & CARE Peaceful community fish which likes plenty of plant cover to hide in. Once settled they become very tame and will even feed out of your fingers.

82°f
▲
70°f

BREEDING Builds a bubble nest including plant material. Male guards the eggs and fry until they are free-swimming.

ORNATE CTENOPOMA *CTENOPOMA ANSORGII*

DESCRIPTION A slender-bodied species with lovely yellow to orange colored body and vertical black stripes. Some fish have a turquoise green body color. This may depend on diet or more likely where it was collected. Maximum size 3 in.

DISTRIBUTION Congo and Zaire.

TEMPERAMENT & CARE Not an aggressive fish but will eat anything it can fit into its mouth. Likes a well-planted aquarium with swimming room at the front. Feed only live and frozen foods.

BREEDING Rarely bred bubble-nester.

82°f
▲
75°f

KISSING GOURAMI *HELOSTOMA TEMMINCKII*

DESCRIPTION A large (1 ft.) gourami which has a compressed body and large forward-pointing lips. The body color is either green or pink depending on the color form, and there is a pearly sheen to it which is very attractive.

DISTRIBUTION Java and Thailand.

TEMPERAMENT & CARE Peaceful species which can be mixed with similar-sized fish. Likes a large aquarium with lots of algae growth on which to browse. Eats all vegetable matter but will also take flake and live foods.

82°f
▲
70°f

BREEDING Spawns under plants at the surface. The eggs float to the surface where the parents ignore them.

PARADISE FISH *MACROPODUS OPERCULARIS*

DESCRIPTION Both sexes are a rusty red with vertical blue bands along the whole body. The gill cover is red with an iridescent blue spot toward the outer edge. Males have longer fins and are brighter colored. Maximum size 4 in.

DISTRIBUTION China, Korea, Malacca, Taiwan, and the Ryukyu Islands.

TEMPERAMENT & CARE Peaceful with other fish, but adult males fight and will kill each other. Although considered a tropical fish, they will live happily at temperatures as low as 59°F.

BREEDING Builds a bubble nest underneath vegetation. After spawning, the male cares for the eggs and young until they are free-swimming.

75°f
▲
59°f

GIANT GOURAMI *OSPHRONEMUS GOURAMI*

DESCRIPTION One of the monsters of the aquarium world, growing up to 2 ft. in body length. When young, the body is brown with darker vertical bands, but as they grow the color fades to a grayish brown without the bands and the lips become very thick and rubbery.

DISTRIBUTION China, India, Java, Malaysia.

TEMPERAMENT & CARE Peaceful enough, but size prohibits inclusion in all but the largest community tank. Likes a lot of vegetable matter in the diet and can be trained to take food from your fingers.

A great fish if you have a large tank.

BREEDING Bubble-nest builder.

THREE SPOT, BLUE, CROSBY, OR GOLD GOURAMI
TRICHOGASTER TRICHOPTERUS

DESCRIPTION There are many different color forms of this fish, ranging from three spotted forms with a blue body to golden fish with a red eye. All have a very large anal fin and their pelvic fins developed into two long "feelers." Maximum size nearly 5 in.

DISTRIBUTION Burma, Malaysia, Sumatra, Thailand, and Vietnam.

TEMPERAMENT & CARE Peaceful with similar-sized fish. Eats all foods and is very hardy. It can tolerate poor water quality and diet better than most other fish.

BREEDING Builds a bubble nest.

Halfbeaks

SUBORDER Exocoetoidei

The halfbeaks belong to a group of fish

that come mainly from marine habitats and include the flying fish.

They have an elongated lower jaw, and the dorsal and anal fins

are positioned towards the rear of the body. They are predators

which feed from the water's surface and have the reputation of being

difficult to maintain in captivity. While some species live in

brackish water, many do not and will suffer if they are kept

in such conditions. Most members of the suborder are egg-layers,

but many species of halfbeak are livebearers or at least

internally fertilize their eggs.

WRESTLING HALFBEAK *DERMOGENYS PUSILLUS*

DESCRIPTION A slender-bodied fish with long lower jaw. The dorsal and anal fins are set well back on the body, and part of the anal fin is modified into a copulatory organ. Maximum size 2 in.

DISTRIBUTION Indonesia, Malaysia, Singapore, and Thailand.

TEMPERAMENT & CARE A peaceful, timid fish which becomes frightened in a community aquarium. Best kept in a species tank with lots of floating plants and hard, alkaline water. Add 1 teaspoon of sea salt per gallon of water. Feeds on live foods at the surface, like fruit flies or mosquito larvae. Can be trained to take carnivore flake food.

81°f
73°f

BREEDING Livebearer which produces fry after a gestation period of about six weeks. Maximum brood size 30.

CELEBES HALFBEAK *NOMORHAMPHUS CELEBENSIS*

DESCRIPTION A slender-bodied fish with a shorter lower jaw than many halfbeaks. The body is yellowish, and the fins have red and black on them. The lower jaw of many males is thickened, black, and turned down. This occurs when the beak has been broken. Maximum size nearly 3 in.

DISTRIBUTION Celebes island, Indonesia.

TEMPERAMENT & CARE A robust species that can live in a community aquarium providing its tankmates are too large to eat. It likes cool, well-oxygenated fresh water. This is a predator which needs lots of live foods in the diet and, despite the mouth shape, will feed off the bottom.

BREEDING Livebearer producing monthly broods of up to 15.

75°f
70°f

Perches

SUBORDER Percoidei

The perches include two groups already

mentioned in this book, the cichlids and labyrinths.

These have been separated from the rest of the suborder

because aquarists look upon them as distinct groups in their

own right. Many of the species in this group have two dorsal fins and

come from brackish or marine habitats. They include the North

American sunfish, which are superb game fish, and some very strange

species with unusual feeding adaptations. On the whole, they are not

kept as aquarium fish, but a couple of important species are

regularly found, so these have been included here.

GLASS FISH *CHANDA RANGA*

81°f
▲
70°f

DESCRIPTION A transparent fish with two dorsal fins and silvery body sac. Apart from a hint of brown in the fins and an electric blue edging to the second dorsal and the anal fin, this is a colorless fish. They are, however, being injected with fluorescent dyes to create garish creatures. No reputable dealer will sell this kind of mutilated fish. Maximum size nearly 3 in.

DISTRIBUTION Bengal, Burma, and India.
TEMPERAMENT & CARE A timid schooling fish that likes some plant cover in the tank. Only keep it with slow-moving fish which will not frighten it. Must be fed some live foods.
BREEDING Lays eggs among plants.

ARCHER FISH *TOXOTES JACULATRIX*

82°f
▲
77°f

DESCRIPTION A robust-bodied fish with a large up-turned mouth, and dorsal and anal fins positioned toward the rear. The body color is silvery with about five blotches along the sides. Maximum size 8 in.

DISTRIBUTION Australia, India, and south-eastern Asia.

TEMPERAMENT & CARE Likes to be kept in a group, but larger fish will bully small ones. Feeds on insects that fall on the water's surface, but if none are forthcoming, they will shoot their own down with jets of water or jump out of the water to catch them. Add 1½ teaspoons of sea salt per gallon of water.

BREEDING Unknown.

Toothcarps – Egglaying

Suborder Cyprinodontoidei, Family Cyprinodontidae

This is a large family of small fresh and brackish-water

fish which are found in most tropical freshwater rivers of the world.

They can even be found in subtropical and cool

temperate regions as well. All have teeth in their jaws but are

generally peaceful fish which will fit in well in a community tank.

Most are straight-forward egg layers which hang their eggs

among plant leaves, but some bury their eggs in mud, and

others carry them around with them for several hours or even weeks

until they hatch. Many species have incredible colors

and make excellent aquarium fish.

LYRETAIL KILLIFISH *APHYOSEMION AUSTRALE*

75°f
▲
70°f

DESCRIPTION A very slender-bodied species with incredibly beautiful coloration. The wild form has a greenish body with red spots and red, yellow, and white fins. Several color forms are known, including gold and chocolate. All the fins are extended but particularly the top and bottom lobes of the tail. Maximum size 2 in.
DISTRIBUTION Africa.

TEMPERAMENT & CARE Peaceful, shy species which likes plenty of plant cover in the aquarium. Males may become pugnacious when breeding, and it is best to keep two or three females to every male.
BREEDING Use soft acidic water for breeding. Hangs eggs among plant leaves close to the substrate, and they take two weeks to hatch.

JAMAICAN KILLIFISH *Cubanichthys pengelleyi*

DESCRIPTION Males are high-backed and deep-bodied fish with large black-edged scales. The body color is golden to bluish with a dark horizontal stripe through the eye to the caudal peduncle. Females are more slender, have smaller fins and lack the blue and gold. Maximum size 2 in.

DISTRIBUTION Jamaica.

TEMPERAMENT & CARE A moderately peaceful fish that can be kept in a community aquarium, providing some plant cover is included. Males are aggressive toward one another; the weaker fish are often bullied to death.

BREEDING Lays a few eggs each day in plants near the substrate. The eggs have a two-week incubation.

77°f
▲
73°f

BLACK-FINNED PEARL FISH *Cynolebias nigripinnis*

DESCRIPTION A stocky-bodied fish with mottled brown females and iridescent bluish-white spotted black males. This is an annual species which grows very quickly to its adult size of just over 1½ in. It will live only a year or so.

DISTRIBUTION Argentina.

TEMPERAMENT & CARE A lively species that can be kept in a community aquarium. Males often squabble and nip each other's fins. Feed live and frozen foods. Keep in moderately hard water with a neutral pH.

73°f
▲
70°f

BREEDING Buries eggs in a peat substrate. The substrate is then removed and kept moist for three months before being put back in water for the eggs to hatch.

AMERICAN FLAGFISH *JORDANELLA FLORIDAE*

75°f
▲
68°f

DESCRIPTION Females are olive with a large black blotch below the origin of the dorsal fin. Males have each scale edged in rusty red and the same blotch as the female. Their dorsal and anal fins are larger and mottled red. Maximum size 2 in.

DISTRIBUTION Coastal regions of North America from Florida southward to the Yucatan peninsula of Mexico.

TEMPERAMENT & CARE Males are aggressive toward one another but otherwise peaceful. Likes some plant cover and will eat all foods.

BREEDING The pair spawn at the base of plant thickets after which the female should be removed. The male guards the eggs and young until they are free-swimming.

RACHOW'S NOTHO *NOTHOBRANCHIUS RACHOVII*

DESCRIPTION Males are truly stunning with a red basic body color overlaid with iridescent blue. The dorsal and anal fins are mottled blue and red. The caudal fin has a band of red, a band of orange, and a thick black edge. Females are a dull gray. Maximum size 2 in.

DISTRIBUTION Africa.

TEMPERAMENT & CARE A peaceful fish, but males are territorial. Can be kept with nonaggressive species. A species tank with a peat substrate is best. Diet should contain lots of live foods.

73°f
▲
70°f

BREEDING Substrate-spawner which needs its eggs kept in moist peat for three months before being placed in water to hatch.

GREEN LAMPEYE *PROCATOPUS ABERRANS*

DESCRIPTION The male has a beautiful blue sheen to his body. The fins are enlarged and blue with red spots. The female tends to be very plain with a silvery gray body and smaller fins. Maximum size 2 in.

DISTRIBUTION Cameroon and Nigeria.

TEMPERAMENT & CARE A peaceful schooling fish that can be kept in any small fish-community aquarium. It likes some plant cover but needs open water areas to swim in as well. Eats all foods.

BREEDING Lays its eggs down cracks in wood or stones but will also place them among the roots of floating plants. They take two weeks to hatch.

79°f
▲
70°f

Toothcarps – Livebearing
SUBORDER Cyprinodontoidei, Families Anablepidae, Goodeidae, & Poeciliidae

This group of fish includes some of the most popular

of all aquarium fish. Most species have the male's anal fin modified

into a copulatory organ so that sperm can be channeled into the

female's vent. Once she has been fertilized, the young take from four

to eight weeks to develop and can be quite large when they are born.

Depending on the species, some females nourish their

young while they are developing. This can be done in a very

rudimentary way with the baby being born the same size as the egg

started out, or it can involve complicated feeding structures

which enable the embryo to grow significantly

during its development.

FOUR-EYED LIVEBEARER *ANABLEPS ANABLEPS*

DESCRIPTION A very odd-looking creature with its eyes divided horizontally so it can see above and below the surface. The body is silvery with a series of longitudinal stripes. Males have a modified anal fin. Maximum size nearly 10 in.

DISTRIBUTION Central America and northern South America.

TEMPERAMENT & CARE A skittish, schooling fish which likes to climb out of the water onto a mud bank to sunbathe. Eats all foods but loves earthworms and other large live foods. Add 1 teaspoonful of sea salt per gallon of water.

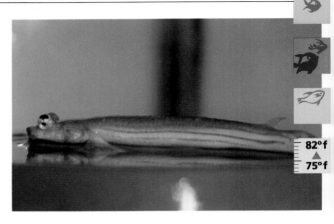

82°f
▲
75°f

BREEDING Livebearer producing up to 15 fry after a six-week gestation period. These are 1¼-2 in. at birth.

PIKE LIVEBEARER *BELONESOX BELIZANUS*

DESCRIPTION A slender fish with large mouth and rows of needle-like teeth. During the day, it is dull brown across the back with a darker midlateral band and a white belly. At night, it turns almost jet black. Maximum size for males nearly 5 in. and females 11 in.

DISTRIBUTION Along the Atlantic coast from Mexico to Honduras.

TEMPERAMENT & CARE A predator that can only be kept with fish which are the same size or larger. Best kept as a pair with a shoal of feeder fish.

BREEDING Females produce broods of up to 250 every month. If the male dies, the female will continue to produce several more broods from stored sperm.

81°f
▲
70°f

RED RAINBOW GOODEID *CHARACODON LATERALIS*

DESCRIPTION Females are green with a row of black spots on the sides of some fish. Males have red fins (the anal with a notch in it) and ventral area with some black spots along the sides and black edging to the fins. Maximum size 2 in.

DISTRIBUTION Springs around the city of Durango, Mexico.

TEMPERAMENT & CARE A peaceful fish which will adapt to a community tank without problems. For breeding it is best kept in a species tank with good plant cover. Feed lots of live food.

73°f
▲
68°f

BREEDING Females produce up to 20 fry every six weeks.

EASTERN MOSQUITO FISH *GAMBUSIA HOLBROOKI*

DESCRIPTION A slender livebearer which has a gray body with a vertical band through the eyes and black speckled fins. Males possess a rod-like anal fin and reach a maximum size of just over 1 in. Females reach 2 in. A black speckled form of this species is known.

DISTRIBUTION Southeastern USA from Florida to the Rio Panuco basin in Mexico. Introduced all over the tropical world for mosquito control.

TEMPERAMENT & CARE A fin-nipper which cannot be kept with other species. Needs a species tank with some plant cover. Feed lots of live foods.

BREEDING Females produce up to 60 fry every four to eight weeks.

86°f
▲
59°f

ONE-SIDED LIVEBEARER *JENYNSIA LINEATA*

DESCRIPTION A slender green fish with black lines and spots along the sides. Males have an anal fin which has been modified into a copulatory organ bent to the left or right. Females have their vent covered on one side. Maximum size, males just over 1½ in., females nearly 3 in.

DISTRIBUTION Argentina and Brazil.

TEMPERAMENT & CARE A peaceful, timid fish which does not thrive in a community aquarium. Prefers a well-planted tank with its own kind. Must have lots of live food in the diet and hard alkaline water.

82°f
▲
73°f

BREEDING After six to eight weeks gestation, the female will produce broods of up to 25 about half an inch long.

HUMPBACK LIMIA *LIMIA NIGROFASCIATA*

DESCRIPTION Both sexes have black vertical bars along the flanks and an overall brownish body fading to white on the stomach. As males mature, they develop a high back and a keel-like edge to the lower body behind the anal fin. Maximum size 2 in.

DISTRIBUTION Lake Miragoane, Haiti.

TEMPERAMENT & CARE Peaceful community fish which fits in well with most other fish of a similar size. Live foods are important to their health, and they should be fed several times a week.

BREEDING Females produce broods of up to 40 every four weeks.

81°f
▲
72°f

ATLANTIC MOLLY *POECILIA MEXICANA*

DESCRIPTION A slender molly with bluish sides and several darker vertical bands along the sides with pale orange in the fins. There is a lot of variation in wild stocks, and this species has been hybridized with other mollies to produce many different color forms. Maximum size 4 in.

DISTRIBUTION Central America.

TEMPERAMENT & CARE Good community fish that will fit in with most other fish providing they are not too timid. Needs neutral to alkaline water conditions and likes plenty of growing plants in the aquarium. For good growth and healthy offspring, feed lots of live foods. Must have clean, well-filtered water.

BREEDING Females produce up to 100 fry every month.

82°f
▲
70°f

GUPPY *POECILIA RETICULATA*

DESCRIPTION The wild-form males are very small fish with a few spots of red, blue, green, or black. From this nondescript fish, hundreds of color forms and fin shapes have been bred. Wild females are gray, but cultivated ones can have larger colored fins as well. Maximum size, males just over 1 in., females 2 in.

DISTRIBUTION Originally Venezuela, Trinidad, and other islands in the area, but now widely distributed throughout the world for mosquito control.

TEMPERAMENT & CARE A hardy fish that does well in a community tank. Do not combine with aggressive fish which may nip the flowing fins. Needs clean, well-filtered water and regular feeds to grow to its full potential.

BREEDING Females produce broods of up to 50 every month.

82°f
▲
64°f

YUCATAN MOLLY *POECILIA VELIFERA*

DESCRIPTION A spectacular animal with a very high and long-based dorsal fin. The body is slate gray to bluish in color, becoming orange on the male's throat. Lots of color forms have been produced by hybridization. Maximum size 6 in.

DISTRIBUTION Yucatan peninsula, Mexico.

TEMPERAMENT & CARE Can be combined with other fish without any problems. For the health of these fish, it is essential that large regular partial water changes are carried out and a good filter is included in the setup.

82°f
▲
73°f

BREEDING Females produce up to 250 fry every month.

GREEN SWORDTAIL *XIPHOPHORUS HELLERI*

DESCRIPTION The commonly found wild form is green with a red stripe running through the eye to the caudal peduncle. The dorsal fin often has red or yellow in it. Males have lower rays of the caudal fin extended into a sword. Many different color forms found in the wild have hybridized in captivity. Lyretail and hi-fin forms are also known. Maximum size 4 in.

DISTRIBUTION Atlantic coastal drainages from Rio Nautla in Mexico to Belize.

TEMPERAMENT & CARE A well-behaved species, but adult males will spar with each other and may become bullies. Need a large well-planted aquarium and a mixed diet including live foods.

BREEDING Females produce up to 250 fry every month.

81°f
▲
70°f

SOUTHERN PLATY *XIPHOPHORUS MACULATUS*

DESCRIPTION A stocky-bodied fish which in the wild generally has a gray body with a few black spots on the sides or in the fins. In captivity they have been developed into hundreds of different color forms plus hi-fin, lyretail and plumetail forms as well. Maximum size 2 in.

DISTRIBUTION Atlantic coastal drainages from Rio Jamapa in Mexico southward to Belize and Guatemala.

TEMPERAMENT & CARE Peaceful community fish which fits in with most other fish.

Generally hardy but will not tolerate poor water quality and dislikes salt in the water.

BREEDING Females produce broods of up to 50 every month.

VARIABLE PLATY *XIPHOPHORUS VARIATUS*

DESCRIPTION A more slender species than the southern platy which, in the wild, is often greenish with black markings and sometimes red in the fins. They have since been developed into a myriad of color forms and hi-fin, lyretail, and plumetail forms as well. Maximum size 2 in.

DISTRIBUTION From the Rio Soto La Marina system southward to the Rio Nautla in Mexico.

TEMPERAMENT & CARE An undemanding fish that will adapt to most conditions well. Eats all foods but takes up to two years to fully develop its coloration.

BREEDING Females produce broods of up to 50 every month.

Rainbow Fish and Silversides

SUBORDER Atherinoidei

Rainbow fish and silversides are a group of rather
small slender fish with comparatively large eyes and two dorsal fins.
Most species are schooling fish which are only really happy
when kept in a group of six or more. They are found throughout
most oceans of the world and in brackish and freshwater habitats,
as well. The species that hobbyists have had most experience with
come from Australia, Celebes, Papua New Guinea, and Madagascar,
but there are others which have yet to make their way into aquarists'
tanks, including several genera from Mexico.

MADAGASCAN RAINBOW FISH *BEDOTIA GEAYI*

DESCRIPTION A beautiful slender-bodied fish with dark midlateral stripe. The dorsal and anal fins are yellowish orange with black edges, and the caudal fin has a black crescent toward the edge which is surrounded with creamy white. Maximum size 5 in.

DISTRIBUTION Madagascar and the surrounding islands.

TEMPERAMENT & CARE Good community fish which likes to live in a group of six or more rainbow fish. Eats all foods but prefers those which float or are in the midwater region.

81°f
72°f

Good filtration and well-oxygenated water are important to its well-being.

BREEDING Lays quite large eggs in plants near the surface.

MACCULLOCH'S RAINBOW FISH *MELANOTAENIA MACCULLOCHI*

DESCRIPTION Overlaying the silvery body color are four or more longitudinal black stripes. These are particularly strong toward the rear of the fish. The fins are orange to reddish. Males have the first dorsal fin longer and more pointed than the female. Maximum size nearly 3 in. Several different species are offered for sale in aquarium stores under this name, but these grow larger and have different coloration.

DISTRIBUTION Australia and Papua New Guinea.

TEMPERAMENT & CARE Schooling fish which does well in the aquarium. Good water quality is important, but

otherwise they are hardy fish which eat anything.

BREEDING Lays eggs in plants near the surface.

75°f
70°f

FORKTAILED BLUE-EYE *Pseudomugil furcatus*

DESCRIPTION A small (almost 2 in.) rainbow fish whose males have the most beautiful coloration. All the fins have bright yellow and black on them, and the throat is a gorgeous orangy yellow. Females are much plainer and lack the throat color.

DISTRIBUTION Papua New Guinea.

TEMPERAMENT & CARE A generally peaceful species, but males will spar from time to time. Ideally keep them in a small group of one male and three females. They like some planted areas in their aquarium but plenty of open swimming areas as well.

77°f
72°f

BREEDING Lays large eggs in plants near the surface. Females only produce one or two eggs per day but spawn every day.

CELEBES RAINBOW FISH *Telmatherina ladigesi*

DESCRIPTION A semi-transparent fish with a gleaming blue stripe running along the rear half of the body. The male's second dorsal and anal fin have extended black fin rays. Otherwise the fins are pale yellow. Maximum size 2½ in.

DISTRIBUTION The island of Celebes, Indonesia.

TEMPERAMENT & CARE A shoaling fish that is always on the move. Likes clean water conditions and aeration in the tank. Will eat all foods from the surface or midwater regions but will ignore food once it has reached the aquarium bottom.

BREEDING Spawns in fine-leafed plants at first light.

81°f
72°f

Other Bony Fishes

The superorder Teleostei (true bony fish)

contains about 10,000 or so species of freshwater fish.

However, only just over 1,000 are regularly seen in the aquarium

trade. Part of the reason for only 10 percent of bony fish being

available is that just over half of the known species either grow too

large or eat a diet that cannot be reproduced in captivity.

This still leaves at least 4,000 species which could be kept

in an aquarium. Despite this wonderful diversity of fish which

could be kept by aquarists, it is interesting to note that statistics

show that 90 percent of aquarium-fish sales are

actually of only 20 species.

PETER'S ELEPHANTNOSE *GNATHONEMUS PETERSII*

DESCRIPTION A strange-looking fish with a long elephant-like trunk which appears to have been stuck on to the head. It has a very thin, elongated caudal peduncle. The body and fins are black except for two vertical lines. Maximum size 8 in.

DISTRIBUTION Cameroon, Nigeria, and Zaire.

TEMPERAMENT & CARE Peaceful with other species but territorial toward its own. Needs a soft substrate and caves to hide in during the day. Sensitive to poor water quality.

81°f
72°f

BREEDING Unknown.

FIRE EEL *MASTACEMBELUS ERYTHROTAENIA*

DESCRIPTION A long eel-like fish with dark body and fiery red stripes. The nose is movable and the nostrils inside tubes are on either side. The dorsal, caudal, and anal fins are joined into one continuous fin. Maximum size 3 ft.

DISTRIBUTION Borneo, Burma, Thailand, and Sumatra.

TEMPERAMENT & CARE This is a nocturnal predator that will eat any fish it can fit in its mouth. It likes to burrow, and the substrate should be sand or fine gravel to accommodate this habit. Feed only live foods.

BREEDING Unknown.

81°f
75°f

AROWANA *OSTEOGLOSSUM BICIRRHOSUM*

DESCRIPTION A slender-bodied, silvery fish with very long-based dorsal and anal fins that almost join up with the tail. The lower jaw has a forked bony protuberance which gives the animal a very odd appearance. Maximum size 4 ft.

DISTRIBUTION Amazon.

TEMPERAMENT & CARE A large predator which will eat any fish small enough to fit in its mouth. Must have a very large tank with plenty of swimming room and some plant cover.

84°f
▲
75°f

BREEDING After spawning, the male looks after the eggs and fry in his mouth for about 55 days. The fry are 4 in. long upon release.

GREEN PUFFERFISH *TETRAODON FLUVIATILIS*

DESCRIPTION A strange-looking fish with beak-like mouth. The body is greenish yellow fading to white on the belly with large black spots. When frightened it sucks in water and puffs its body up like a balloon. Maximum size 6 in.

DISTRIBUTION Southeast Asia.

TEMPERAMENT & CARE An aggressive fish which may only be kept with bigger fish and never with its own species. Eats all live foods but loves snails which it crunches up with its beak. Add 1 teaspoonful of sea salt per gallon of water.

BREEDING Lays its eggs in a pit. The male protects them until the fry are able to take care of themselves.

81°f
▲
75°f

A

Abramites hypselonotus 36
American Flagfish 65
Anableps anableps 68
Ancistrus dolichopterus 29
Angelfish 48
Anostomus anostomos
(Striped Anostomus) 36
Aphocharax anisitsi 37
Aphyosemion australe 62
Apistogramma nijsseni 43
Archer Fish 9, 61
Arowana 79
Astronotus ocellatus 43
Astyanax fasciatus mexicanus 37

B

Balantiocheilus melanopterus 15
Barbus oligolepis
(Checker Barb) 9, 15
Barbus schwanefeldi
(Tinfoil Barb) 16
Barbus semifasciolatus
(Schuberti Barb) 17
Barbus tetrazona
(Tiger Barb) 17
Barbus titteya
(Cherry Barb) 12, 18
Bedotia geayi 75
Belonesox belizanus 68
Betta splendens 53
Bitterling 27
Bloodfin 37
Botia macracanthus 18
Botia sidthimunki
(Chain Botia) 19
Brachydanio rerio 19
Brachygobius xanthozona 51

C

Carnegialla strigata strigata 38
Carassius auratus 6, 20
Catfish, Bristle-nose 33
Catfish Ghost 33
Catfish, Polka-dot 34
Catfish, Whiptail 31
Chanda ranga 60
Characodon lateralis 69
Cichlid, Dwarf Panda 43
Cichlid, Jewel 44
Cichlid, Lyretail 45
Cichlid, Regan's Julie 45
Cichlid, Striped Pike 44
Colisa lalia 54
Corydoras aeneus
(Bronze Corydoras) 29
Corydoras barbatus
(Banded Corydoras) 30
Corydoras paleatus
(Peppered Corydoras) 31
Crenicichla strigata 44
Ctenopoma ansorgii 54

Cubanichthys pengellyi 64
Cynolebias nigripinnis 64

D

Danio, Zebra 19
Danio aequipinnatus
(Giant Danio) 20
Dermogenys pusillus 58
Discus, Green 49

E

Elephantnose, Peter's 78
Epalzeorhynchus bicolor 21
Epalzeorhynchus kallopterus 22

F

Farlowella acus 31
Fire Eel 78
Flying Fox 22

G

Gambusia holbrooki 69
Glass Fish 60
Gnathonemus petersii 78
Goby, Bumblebee 51
Goby, Peacock 51
Goldfish 6, 20
Goodeid, Red Rainbow 69
Gourami, Dwarf 54
Gourami, Giant 54
Gourami, Honey 11
Gourami, Kissing 55
Gourami, Ornate 54
Gourami, Three Spot/
Crosby/Gold 56
Guppy, Yucatan 72
Gymnocorrymbus ternetzi 38
Gyrinocheilus aymonieri 22

H

Halfbeak, Celebes 58
Halfbeak, Wrestling 58
Harlequin 25
Hatchetfish, Marbled 38
Headstander, Marbled 36
Helostoma temminckii 55
Hemichromis bimaculatus 44
Hoplosternum thoracatum
(Spotted Hoplo) 32
Hyphessobrycon herbertaxelrodi
39
Hypostomus punctatus 32

J

Jenynsia lineata 70
Jordanella floridae 65
Julidochromis regani 45

K

Killifish, Jamaican 64
Killifish, Lyretail 63
Knifefish 8
Kribensis 47
Kryptopterus bicirrhis 33

L

Labyrinth fish 52
Lampeye, Green 66

Leuciscus idus 23
Limia nigrofasciata 70
Livebearer, Four-eyed 68
Livebearer, One-sided 70
Livebearer, Pike 68
Loach, Chinese Weather 23
Loach, Clown 18
Loach, Coolie 23
Loach, Sucking 22

M

Macropodus opercularis 6, 55
Mastacembelus erythrotaenia 78
Mbuna, Auratus 46
Mbuna, Zebra 48
Melanochromis auratus 46
Melanotaenia maccullochi 75
Minnow, White Cloud
Mountain 27
Misgurnus anguillicaudatus 23
Molly, Atlantic 71
Mosquito Fish, Eastern 69

N

Nematobrycon palmeri 39
Neolamprologus brichardi 45
Nomorhamphus celebensis 58
Nothobranchius rachovii
(Rachow's Notho) 66
Notropis lutrensis 24

O

Orfe 23
Oscar 43
Osphronemus gourami 56
Osteoglossum bicirrhosum 79

P

Panaque suttoni 33
Pangio kuhlii sumatranus 24
Papiliochromis ramirezi 46
Paracheirodon innesi 40
Paradise Fish 6, 55
Pearl Fish, Black-finned 64
Pelvicachromis pulcher 47
Piranha, Red-bellied 41
Phenacogrammus interruptus
41
Platy, Southern 73
Platy, Variable 73
Plecostomus 32
Plecostomus, Blue-eyed 33
Poecilia mexicana 71
Poecilia reticulata 71
Poecilia velifera 72
Procatopus aberrans 66
Pseudomugil furcatus 76
Pseudotropheus zebra 48
Pterophyllum scalare 48
Pufferfish, Green 79

R

Rainbow Fish, Celebes 12, 26
Rainbow Fish, Forktail
Blue-eye 76

Rainbow Fish, MacCulloch's
75
Rainbow Fish, Madagascar 75
Ram 46
Rasbora heteromorpha 25
Rasbora trilineatus 26
Rasbora urophthalma
(Exclamation Spot
Rasbora) 26
Red Shiner 24
Rhodeus sericeus amerus 27

S

Scissortail 26
Serrasalmus nattereri 41
Shark, Red-tailed black 21
Shark, Silver 15
Siamese Fighting Fish 53
Silversides 74
Swordtail, Green 72
Symphysodon aequifasciatus 49
Synodontis angelicus 34

T

Tanichthys albonubes 27
Tateurndina ocellicauda 51
Telmatherina ladigesi 12, 76
Tetra, Black Neon 39
Tetra, Black Widow 38
Tetra, Blind Cave 37
Tetra, Congo 41
Tetra, Emperor, 39
Tetra, Neon 40
Tetraodon fluviatilis 79
Toxotes jaculatrix 61
Trichogaster trichopterus 56

X

Xenopoecilus sarasorium
10, 11
Xiphophorus helleri 72
Xiphophorus maculatus 73
Xiphophorus variatus 73

Picture Credits

The Goldfish Bowl, Oxford:
pp. 6, 8, 9, 15, 16, 17
(bottom), 18, 19(b), 20(b),
21–5, 26 (top), 27(b), 30, 31,
32(b), 33, 34, 36–8, 40,
41(b), 43–5, 46(t), 47–9, 51,
53, 54(b), 55, 56, 58, 60, 61,
63, 64(b), 65, 78, 79.

Derek J. Lambert: pp. 10, 11,
17(t), 19(t), 20(t), 26(b),
27(t), 29, 32(t), 39, 41(t),
46(b), 54(t), 64(t), 66, 68, 69,
70–3, 75, 76.